LIBERATING THE MEDIA

THE NEW JOURNALISM

LIBERATING THE MEDIA

THE NEW JOURNALISM

by CHARLES C. FLIPPEN

BEN H. BAGDIKIAN
ARTHUR BARRON
JEROME BARRON
BRIAN BOYER
RON DORFMAN
ERNEST IMHOFF
JAY JENSEN

THEODORE F. KOOP
LESTER MARKEL
JACK NEWFIELD
NEAL ROSENAU
ROBERT B. SEMPLE, JR.
GAY TALESE
TOM WOLFE

ACROPOLIS BOOKS ON CURRENT ISSUES

Published by ACROPOLIS BOOKS LTD. ● WASHINGTON, D.C. 20009

CONTEMPORARY ISSUES IN JOURNALISM
Volume I: Politics and the Press
Volume II: Why Aren't We Getting Through?
Volume III: The Political Image Merchants
Volume IV: Liberating the Media: The New Journalism
Volume V: The Super Journalists

© Copyright 1974, Charles C. Flippen II

This book developed from the "Baltimore Sun Distinguished Lecture Series," a project of the College of Journalism, University of Maryland. The lectures were made possible by a grant from the A. S. Abell Company Foundation and the Baltimore Sunpapers.

Special gratitude is due to Mr. William F. Schmick, Jr., President of the A. S. Abell Company Foundation; Mr. Perry J. Bolton, Assistant to the President of the Foundation; and Mr. Philip S. Heisler, Managing Editor of the Baltimore Evening Sun, who were instrumental in getting the Lecture Series started.

The purpose of the Lecture Series is to provide a forum for the expression of ideas by distinguished journalists, scholars of journalism, and others, and to provide a continuing medium of education and exchange between the Journalism College, its students and alumni, and the journalism profession.

Grateful acknowledgement is made for permission to reprint the following selections:
"The Noonday Underground," reprinted with the permission of Farrar, Straus & Giroux, Inc. from THE PUMP HOUSE GANG by Tom Wolfe, copyright © 1968 by Tom Wolfe, copyright © 1966 by the World Journal Tribune Corporation, Copyright © 1964, 1965, 1966 by the New York Herald Tribune Inc.
Selection from HONOR THY FATHER reprinted by permission of The World Publishing Company from HONOR THY FATHER by Gay Talese, Copyright © 1971 by Gay Talese.
"Tisch Gang: the City's Permanent Government," by Jack Newfield, reprinted by permission of Jack Newfield. Photo of page 1, July 3, 1969 issue of the Village Voice, also reproduced by permission of Mr. Newfield.
"No Cease-Fire in Chicago Press," by Neal Rosenau, reprinted from Chicago Journalism Review with permission of the publisher. Copyright © 1973 by Association of Working Press, Inc. Photo of page 1, May 1972 issue also reproduced by permission of the publisher.
"Network Television and the Personal Documentary," by Arthur Barron, reprinted by permission from Film Comment, volume 6 number 1. Copyright © 1970 Film Comment Publishing Corporation, all rights reserved.
Still photographs from the Films "Eat," "Dog Star Man Part 1: The Art of Vision," "Dog Star Man Part II," "Guns of the Trees," and "Reminiscences of a Journey to Lithuania" are from the Anthology Film Archives and are reproduced by permission.

ACROPOLIS BOOKS LTD.
Colortone Building, 2400 17th St., N.W., Washington, D.C. 20009

Printed in the United States of America by
COLORTONE PRESS, Creative Graphics Inc.
Washington, D.C. 20009

Library of Congress Catalog Number 73-22086

Standard Book No. 87491-361-6 (cloth)
87491-362-4 (paper)

Library of Congress Cataloging in Publication Data
Main entry under title:

Liberating the media: the new journalism.

Based mainly on a series of lectures held in the spring of 1972 at College Park, Md., and sponsored by the Baltimore Sunpapers and the College of Journalism, University of Maryland.
Bibliography: p.
1. Journalism—Addresses, essays, lectures.
I. Flippen, Charles C., ed.
PN4724.L5   070   73-22086
ISBN 0-87491-376-4
ISBN 0-87491-377-2 (pbk.)

CIP

Contents

Preface / 7

1 The New Journalism / 9
Charles C. Flippen

2 The New Journalism In Historical Perspective / 18
Jay Jensen

3 The Noonday Underground from The Pump House Gang / 29
Tom Wolfe

4 The Book As a Medium for Journalism / 42
from a discussion with Gay Talese

5 Selection from Honor Thy Father / 50
Gay Talese

6 The "Truth" About Objectivity and the New Journalism / 59
Jack Newfield

7 Tisch Gang from The Village Voice / 67
Jack Newfield

8 Objective Journalism / 76
Lester Markel

9 The Necessity of Conventional Journalism:
A Blend of the Old and the New / 85
Robert B. Semple, Jr.

10 The Underground Press:
Notes on the Past and the Future / 93
Brian Boyer

11 Selections from the Underground Press / **105**
"Gay Pride Week" *Harry,* July 17, 1970 / **107**

"Confessions of a Sexploited Lady"
Berkeley Tribe, August 23-29, 1969 / **108**

"HARRY Reporter Drops Acid, Hears Billy Graham,
Sees Apocalypse, Digs It" *Harry,* July 17, 1970 / **113**

12 Democracy in the Newsroom: Notes on the Movement
Toward Non-Seigneurial Journalism / **118**
Ron Dorfman

13 No Cease-fire in Chicago Press *Chicago Journalism
Review,* May, 1973 / **125**
Neal Rosenau

14 Editorial Control in the Newsroom / **138**
Ernest Imhoff

15 Personal Journalism in Television / **145**
Theodore F. Koop

16 Network Television and the Personal Documentary
Film Comment, Spring, 1970 / **152**
Arthur Barron

17 The Underground Film / **162**
Charles C. Flippen

18 Public Access to the Media and its Critics / **173**
Jerome Barron

19 Considerations on the Future of American Journalism / **192**
Ben H. Bagdikian

Bibliography / **203**

Index / **209**

Preface

This book had as its starting point a lecture series held in the spring of 1972 at College Park, Maryland. The purpose of the series was to investigate the hazily defined and somewhat controversial area known as the New Journalism. I was interested in considering both the various manifestations of what might be called the New Journalism and its influence on mainstream or traditional journalism. In preparing the book I have added several items which were not part of the original series in the hope that the book might be more useful and, perhaps, more entertaining to its readers. The introductory overview and the chapter on the underground film by the editor are new. The chapter by Arthur Barron is reprinted from *Film Comment*. Additionally a number of illustrative chapters have been added. The chapters by Jay Jensen, Gay Talese, Jack Newfield, Lester Markel, Robert Semple, Brian Boyer, Ron Dorfman, Ernest Imhoff, Theodore Koop, Jerome Barron and Ben Bagdikian are edited versions of lectures given as part of the series.

This series was the fourth in an annual series of lectures sponsored by the *Baltimore Sunpapers* and the College of Journalism, University of Maryland. The editor wishes to thank the Sunpapers and the A.S. Abell Company Foundation for their financial support of the series. Additionally thanks go to my colleagues on the faculty of the College of Journalism for their aid. Special appreciation is expressed to Drs. Richard Lee and Lee Brown for their suggestions and assistance. Also my thanks to Nick Miles and Dan Webster for photographic assistance and to Anju Chaudhary who typed much of the manuscript. Finally, and most greatly, my appreciation goes to my wife, Edia, for her always thoughtful aid.

C.C.F.

1 | The New Journalism

By Charles C. Flippen

THERE IS A RANGY, white-haired gentleman I know of, a self-proclaimed savant in the realm of journalism education. To look upon this man one would think he had reached the age of contentment. Yet let someone mention the new term New Journalism, or even use in print the initials NJ, and he is ready to do pen and ink battle with that person.

"No such thing," he will tell you with great conviction—perhaps even a touch of ferocity. "There's nothing new about the New Journalism."

There are many who take this position and are ready, typing paper at hand, to prove their point. Curiously, even some who are labelled New Journalists themselves deny with vigor the existence of such an entity.

Consider, if you will, the following. It is the lead or beginning of an article which appeared in the *Washington Post* on January 3, 1958, page 1:

"It seemed like a nightmare . . ."

Bernard J. Mainer, 28-year-old blind pianist, lay critically wounded at Emergency Hospital yesterday and recalled the night a week ago when three men were shot at the J-Del Tavern on 9th St., N.W.

This was about as creative as one could be in those days in a news story or news-feature. (If you missed the "creativity," it began with a quote instead of just the facts.)

Now look at the following, again from the *Washington Post* page 1, dated February 25, 1973:

Dripping blood, her ears ringing from the three bullets that had been fired into her head, Almira Khaalis staggered into the bedroom and saw her 10-year-old brother, Rahman, shot to death on the bed.

She touched her hand to him and said, "Bismillah" (the name of Allah or God). She then found her brother, Daud, 25, also shot to death. She placed her hand on him and said, "Bismillah."

She then wandered, half-dazed, around the house to find five other persons dead, including her 18-month-old daughter Khadyja, who was drowned.

Almira Khaalis, 23, in an interview yesterday, calmly gave an account of the bloody events of Jan. 18 when as many as eight men broke into the Hanafi Moslem headquarters, at 7700 16th St. N.W. and killed seven persons and wounded two others.

Something has happened. One might be able to argue that there is no such thing as The New Journalism, but that there is something new in journalism no one can deny. That something is a new freedom to express oneself, a new liberation, a new concern with the individual such as did not exist fifteen years ago. The lead on the 1973 story would have been unthinkable in 1958.

The term New Journalism is an umbrella term. It means different things to different people. Some go so far as to say it means anything new or out of the ordinary in journalism. But there are, I believe, about five items which constitute and provide for this new aura of journalism.

These may be labelled:

1. Literary Journalism
2. Advocacy Journalism

3. Underground Journalism
4. Democracy in the Newsroom
5. Public Access

(Some add a sixth category, occasionally known as precision journalism,[1] by which they mean the use of social science research techniques by journalists. Unquestionably this is new to journalism. But I would not call it a part of the New Journalism because it does not contribute to the new concern for individual expression.)

Literary Journalism—Most who discuss the New Journalism think first, and sometimes only, of what I have called literary journalism. By this is meant the use of sophisticated literary techniques, such as are usually associated with fiction, in journalistic writing. Those who attempt to debunk the newness of this kind of journalism say that writers of the past also applied literary techniques to journalism. And indeed it is possible to go back to the man some call the first modern journalist, Daniel Defoe, and find among his work pieces which, if they appeared today, would be called by some New Journalism. *A Journal of the Plague Year* is perhaps the most obvious example. It is most definitely a literary treatment of a real event.

Frequently mentioned as an early example of this kind of literary journalism is a piece by the 19th century essayist William Hazlitt called "The Fight." In this article Hazlitt records his reactions to the prize-fight—it is not unlike some of the journalistic work of Norman Mailer. Other writers often called pre-New Journalists include Mark Twain, George Bernard Shaw and Ernest Hemingway. Hemingway, for example, in *Green Hills of Africa* attempted to write of a true event (a big game hunt) in novel-like format. Truman Capote, who thought he was producing a new art form, actually did something of the same thing with *In Cold Blood.*

Yet there are several things which could be considered new about current literary journalism. For one thing, there is quantity. Literary journalism has become part of mainstream journal-

[1] See Everette Dennis, ed., *The Magic Writing Machine,* Eugene, Oregon, 1971.

ism. One has only to look at any of a number of major contemporary journals to see it practiced extensively. This was not the situation earlier. Second, some would argue that the literary techniques currently being applied to journalism are far more sophisticated than those of earlier journalists—including such things as composite characterization, interior monologue and even a kind of stream of consciousness. Finally, Tom Wolfe has argued, vigorously, that one important difference is in purpose— that current literary journalists are serious reporters who only use literary techniques in conveying information. He feels that many of the earlier writers alluded to in this context were engaging primarily in literary exercises.[2]

Advocacy Journalism—If one does not think of literary journalism as the New Journalism, then one is likely to think of advocacy journalism. Some times advocacy and literary journalism are thought of as a package which makes up the New Journalism because they are often practiced simultaneously—though not always. Advocacy in journalism basically refers to the journalist, the reporter injecting his view point or opinion into his writing— not in editorials or columns, but in feature articles and even news stories. Such open advocacy in journalism is in direct opposition to what had become the traditional and accepted role of the journalist as more-or-less objective observer and conveyor of information. Whether or not the role of advocate is legitimate for the reporter is one of the most serious questions in American journalism today.

Of course, no one argues that advocacy journalism is new. During the 18th and 19th centuries the American press was often virulently opinionated. In the late 18th century, during the period of the political press, and through much of the 19th century open advocacy was the norm, the expected. Often newspapers were supported by political interests and were expected to trumpet those interests. Just as often independent editors had their own

---

[2] Tom Wolfe, "Why They Aren't Writing the Great American Novel Anymore," *Esquire*, December, 1972, pp. 152-159, 272-280.

12

pet causes for which they fought in their columns. Gradually during the latter part of the 19th century and into the 20th because of social and technological factors the press began to become more objective. Today what we call objective journalism has become the norm in this country and the push apparently to return to older ways raises not only fury but fear.

Those who proclaim advocacy usually do so for one of two reasons. First, they argue—rightfully—that objectivity is impossible. Our minds are like prisms shaped by our past experiences; in turn, everything we observe is also shaped by this prism. They go on to argue that the reporter is fooling himself and his audience if he thinks differently—that it would be better for him to recognize and proclaim his biases and prejudices and write from them. Thus he would be neither self-deceiving nor deceiving the audience. The second argument of the advocacy journalists is that traditional journalism has led the press to overlook social ills and injustices and to accept official mendacity. The most commonly pointed to example is the "red scare" period of the 1950's when most of the press unquestioningly accepted the lies of Senator Joseph McCarthy about communists in government because he was an "official." And it was proper, objective journalism to report what officials said.

Those who hold that objective—or, perhaps better, balanced—journalism ought to remain the mainstream generally accede to the arguments of the advocates. Yes, most would agree, pure objectivity in journalism is not possible. But this does not mean the effort ought to be abandoned. Is it not better to attempt to be objective or at least fair than to give up the effort all together simply because some pristine form is not attainable? Would we truly be better served if all journalists were openly cause-oriented? Most would also admit to past inadequacies or failings of the press. But in general these have been the result of a failure to use properly traditional journalistic techniques not the result of a failure to be advocates. Most proponents of traditional journalism would also go a step further and say that there is a place, indeed a need, for advocacy in the media, but that it ought not to become the central thrust of American journalism.

13

Underground Journalism—The last three elements which I have listed as components of the New Journalism—underground journalism, democracy in the newsroom and the right of public access—are not central to what most think of when they consider the New Journalism. They are not any less important; they are, rather, contributory to the atmosphere which makes possible the New Journalism. The underground press was and is made up of many kinds of publications and people. These include political extremists—both left and right—who seek only a place from which to harangue, sexual crazies who only want to do their thing in print, and serious journalists who for one reason or another found the establishment press to be too restrictive. The impetus for this press was the same that in other times drove people to pamphleteering or to occasionally setting up their own counter press. It was and is the desire or need to say something particular in print. The differences between earlier and more recent underground journalists are that during the last decade there seemed to be more of them, they may have been more blatant and they became labelled. Their importance lies in that fact that, among other things, they showed the establishment that the world would not end if certain things appeared in print—that, in some instances, it might even be a better place—and that upon occasion this sort of thing could even make a profit. In other words, they helped make ready the way for much of what is new in the establishment press today. Several of the better of the underground publications—those which are still producing after some years—have in many instances become almost establishment themselves. And most major newspapers have in their newsrooms today people who got their first exposure to journalism with the undergrounds or college papers—which in the late sixties were often carbons of the undergrounds. The liberating influence was inevitable.

We find the same sort of occurrences among the other underground media—notably in the film.

Democracy in the Newsroom—With the possible exception of some underground papers, democracy in the newsroom remains largely a goal of New Journalists rather than an accomplishment. Generally, the journalists interested in this goal are seeking a greater voice in the editorial policies of the newsroom and more control over their own functioning as journalists. The essence of their argument is that if journalists are professionals, and they definitely believe themselves to be such, then they ought to be treated by their employers as professionals, not hired hands— that is, they ought to be freed to function as their training, talents and intellects tell them they ought. Those who propose this position feel that the total journalistic product would be improved if they were allowed to function in this manner. Those who oppose this view argue that any organization if it is to function, particularly if it is to function efficiently, must have structure and structure implies lines of authority. Without structure chaos could ensue, and no newspaper could long function in a chaotic situation.

Such dreams of individual freedom are not new, of course. Though progress has been made in this direction, the complete achievement of the goal seems not very close. This has led some journalists to turn to other outlets for those things which the restricting circumstances of the usual newspaper would not allow. In some instances this has meant work with or the establishment of media reviews—sheets which publish the journalism that the major media won't, and which also criticize the media. Another effort of journalists who seek this kind of democracy is an attempt to draft a kind of Declaration of Independence or Bill of Rights for reporters. This effort is nascent and therefore it is too early to speak of results. But it, like the media reviews, tells the editor and the publisher that the reporter is not a lackey and this, too, is liberating.

Public Access to the Media—Many do not see this last category as part of the New Journalism—primarily because the impetus for public access has come from without rather than from within the media. Yet this most definitely is part of the new thrust, the new aura of journalism. Public access refers to the belief among a growing number of people that the public has certain rights in the media—and that among these rights is access in one form or another to the pages or the airwaves for expressions of views from the public. The demands for increased access vary from the legalistic to the moralistic—from the contention that the public has a First Amendment right to the media to the notion that the media ought to do it because it is right. The desires and suggestions include the expansion of the letters to the editor column to one or two pages, accepting guest columns of opinion, and accepting all advertising. No matter what they desire specifically all who argue for this position agree that the media have not been responsive to the public—unless economic gains or losses were involved. The media have been quick enough to censor or to pander in response to public views (or assumed public views) when they sensed that money was involved. But at least partially because money and numbers are not involved in the public access issue the media have not been responsive generally except when forced—as by the Federal Communications Commission in its Fairness Doctrine. Nonetheless continuing demands and pressure from the public—even a small portion of the public—make themselves felt, make the media masters a bit more aware of the true nature of their audiences. And this, also, becomes an influence for change.

Conclusion

The New Journalism is here, is with us, is real and, in its total effect as well as some of its parts, is *new*. To deny this is to deny the evidence before our eyes. One has only to look at our major newspapers and magazines to see that something different *is* being printed and that there is a new spirit in journalism. There is a freshness, a vigor, an exuberance, a freedom, a concern for the individual which was not possible before in the mass media.

The highly individualistic writing styles of journalists such as Tom Wolfe and Gay Talese would not have been considered feasible in the journalistic milieu of an earlier time. Today their works are eagerly sought by the major media and their progeny encouraged by even non-major publications.

Without becoming alarmist about it, one ought to say that there are dangers involved in the New Journalism. If the New Journalism were to become the mode of American journalism we would have lost something very valuable—the tradition of objective or impartial journalism. While many sins can be attributed to traditional journalism, while one can agree that ideals are unattainable—is it not better to strive for such ideals as objective or fair reporting than to abandon the goal altogether? Do we truly want all our news from the New Journalists? Of course, we are not yet about to see the New Journalism engulf us. Traditional, objective writing is still the mainstream of American journalism. But incursions have been made. Many newspapers are accepting the more personal approach in certain areas—particularly in feature writing. And there are several major magazines which publish virtually nothing but New Journalism.

So far it is all to the good. American journalism needed something to free it from the restrictive, formulistic mode it had acquired. Some, of course, feel the New Journalism has taken us too far; others feel not far enough. In either case, new life has been stirred, creativity engendered. The question now becomes, shall the center hold?

2 The New Journalism in Historical Perspective

By Jay Jensen

ONE OF THE MOST FAMOUS essays of the 19th century writer, William C. Hazlitt, was "The Fight," written in 1822. One of the fighters, "Gas-man" Hickman, was only five feet nine inches tall and weighed about 170 pounds. His opponent, William Bill Neate, was six feet and weighed 200 pounds. They fought some 18 rounds before Hickman finally could not make it for the next.

Hazlitt did not write the essay in the way we are accustomed to reading reports on fights. The typical report that comes over the wire today gives the reader the results, a round-by-round account, and comments from people as to the strategy employed in the fight. The loser is usually asked "Did he hurt you?" and he will say "Naw, not really." This is the common format of both broadcast and written reports on fighting.

But Hazlitt wrote about the fight as what today would be called a "happening." He was mainly interested in *being at* the fight and *being witness* to the fight. He knew nothing about fighting, but it is clear that he found it terribly fascinating. And his approach was very much like that of Tom Wolfe and other New Journalists, who strive more to tell us what it is like to "be there" than to tell us what happened.

It is worth noting that Norman Mailer's first venture into journalism was his report of the first Liston-Patterson fight. The article appeared in *Esquire* magazine, a seedbed of New Journalism. Previously, in 1959, Mailer had written in *Advertisements of Myself* some of his ideas *about* journalism, but this was his first foray *into* journalism. What came out of that particular piece on the Liston-Patterson fight was what can fairly be called an "essay on existentialism," as much as a piece of journalism. And, of course, this is not surprising, as existentialism is something that Mailer is very much interested in; indeed, he regards himself as an existentialist.

Anyway, the point is the flavor and the attitude of the Mailer piece and Tom Wolfe-type reporting and Hazlitt's piece on the fight in 1822 are quite similar.

Incidentally, George Bernard Shaw also reported on a fight once, the Beckett-Carpenter fight, in *Nation* magazine in 1919, and his approach was essentially the same. He described, or tried to describe, what it was like *to be at* a fight. He himself was astonished at what fights were like, and that is what he wrote about. As in Hazlitt's case, the reader did find out who won, but the writer's main purpose was to describe what it was like *to be there.*

A favorite put down, using such examples, is to say that the New Journalism is not "new," that it is only borrowing and reviving old techniques. But one cannot dispose of the New Journalism in such a simple way, because old techniques are constantly being revived and used in new ways under new circumstances. This is what has actually happened in the case of the New Journalism, so it seems quite legitimate to call it "new" in that sense—new in the sense that it is something different from what we have been used to, and something that apparently has been accepted as journalism of a sort.

There are a number of prominent names associated with the New Journalism. One of the most famous is Truman Capote, author of *In Cold Blood*, which he describes as a "non-fiction novel." He had talked about doing such a work as early as 1954, though it was not until the sensational Clutter mass murder in

1959 that he had a topic. He did not publish *In Cold Blood* until 1966; for that reason it has been a little difficult for some to think of Capote's effort as journalism, as it was reporting seven years after the event.

Another famous name closely associated with the New Journalism is, of course, Mailer. Norman Mailer is a novelist; some regard him as America's foremost novelist. More than a few call him a genius; others call him a neurotic. He is, in any case, extraordinarily creative, and he thinks about things in ways that ordinary journalists would not think about them.

Mailer is, I'd say, fundamentally a metaphysician, an existentialist metaphysician, which makes him, as much as anything, a philosopher of sorts who just happens to have taken up journalism. He himself became dissatisfied with the novel as a form of expression some years before he fully attempted journalism. One of the things he said very early in talking about journalism was that reporting on events and reporting what people said and did, and things that you did not approve of or you did not believe, corrupted the journalist. Mailer felt that it was possible to do something about that and he felt he would try to do it.

And so we have had since that time two works by Mailer that he wrote as pieces of journalism and have come to be thought of as New Journalism. One was *Miami and the Seige of Chicago* and the other was the *Armies of the Night*. The latter was published in *Harper's* and then in book form, and won the Pulitzer prize. The *Armies of the Night* dealt with the march on the Pentagon, in which he was directly involved; *Miami and the Seige of Chicago* reported the Miami and the Chicago Republican and Democratic conventions.

Another name associated with this movement is Gay Talese. His has become one of the more prominent names, mainly because of his most recent book, *Honor Thy Father*. The one that brought him instant fame, however, was his study of *The New York Times, The Kingdom and the Power*. The techniques he used were not new, but he used them on topics and subjects in ways that we were not accustomed to. Recently, Talese has expressed a kind of reluctance to be classified as a New Journalist. Why, I am not sure. He surely is associated with the movement, and he is so identified by some because of his use of the technique of internal monologue. In this type of writing you do research, you set up a situation and, though you are not really sure what the man thought, you figure out that, given the circumstances, he must have thought such and such a thing, so you write it as though he did in fact think it. In that sense it becomes fiction, but presumably it is based upon sufficient facts so that it is somewhere between a novel and journalism.

A fourth major figure is Tom Wolfe, a French impressionist among the New Journalists. Impressionism, whether we are talking about painting or literature, is depicting the world of ephemeral appearance, revealing, as in a series of snapshots or glances, what the eye or the mind sees from instant to instant. The concentration is upon features or characteristics rather than the structure or the form of events. This is the definition of French Impressionism in painting in the late 19th century associated with Monet, Cezanne, Degas and Renoir. They were not interested in structure and form, but in recording impressions of light striking surfaces of objects under varying conditions. In literature, we had much the same kind of movement. In writing, it is the uncritical expression of the hyper-aesthetic sensations produced by the external world. It results in an intensely nervous style, which makes one think immediately of Tom Wolfe—a very nervous writer. One of Wolfe's characteristics is a kind of picturesque virtuosity; that is, he shows all of his talents all of the time, or at least he tries to. And he has little regard generally with form or clarity—which is not to say that he is obscure, for that is not his purpose. But he certainly does not write in inverted pyramid form; nor does he use block structure. He seems not to care much about structure as such.

In the United States, in poetry, this kind of approach is associated with the names of Ezra Pound and Carl Sandburg; in prose, with Sherwood Anderson and John Dos Passos. So it is true that what Tom Wolfe has been doing is not new in the sense that he created it or invented it, but it is new in the sense that it is something quite different from what we have been used to now for a number of years and have regarded as journalism. And this, basically, is what for me is "new" about the New Journalism, whatever approach it takes or techniques it uses.

Edwin Emery, in his *The Press and America*, refers to the journalism of Joseph Pulitzer in the late 19th century as a New Journalism. If we take that tack, we find that New Journalism appears again and again and again. Michael Johnson, a professor of English, makes an elaborate definition or description of what he means by New Journalism and he means not just the major stylists, such as Capote, Mailer, Talese, and Wolfe. He also includes the "underground press." He includes "rock journalism" and "underground radio" and what he calls the "new muckraking." It is a very broad definition of the New Journalism. My purpose, however, will be to discuss New Journalism only in the sense associated with the names of people like Mailer, Capote, Tom Wolfe, and Gay Talese.

Truman Capote talked about the New Journalism as a nonfiction novel. Norman Mailer, in his *Armies of the Night*, entitled the first section "History as a Novel," which was, in effect, a history of himself. That is, he told what happened to him. The second section he called "Novel as History" and this was supposed to be what happened—quite apart from himself. Tom Wolfe says that New Journalism is what he and Jimmy Breslin, Dick Schaap and a few others from the *Herald Tribune* were trying to do. They were dissatisfied with traditional journalism and they started doing other things. In effect, he is saying that the New Journalism is Me or Us. And in many ways, I suppose, that is true.

Charles Brown, of Pennsylvania State University, one of the foremost scholars among journalism educators, calls the New Journalism simply the "new art" of journalism. His explanation, basically, is that it is much the situation that Byron and Shelley found themselves in. The poetic drama was dead, so they had to write something else. And so today some writers believe the novel in our time is dead and this is the era of journalism, an often repeated phrase. Even Gore Vidal has written some extraordinary journalism, based primarily upon his talents as a writer.

A lot of these writers who have taken to journalism are certainly not in the traditional sense "reporters" and, indeed, they are often in the traditional sense very bad reporters. Norman Mailer, for example, in *Miami and the Seige of Chicago*, from the standpoint of the newsroom or the headquarters of the AP in New York, would have been thought of as having "missed the story" most of the time. But, on the other hand, he does give a picture of the conventions, both in Miami and in Chicago, that one would not find ordinarily in a newspaper or even a magazine, much less radio or TV.

This raises the immediate point, too, that most of the New Journalism is found not in the newspapers but in the magazines. There have been some attempts to use the techniques in newspapers, sometimes with disastrous results. And mainly, I think, because of two factors. One is that there is just not enough space in the newspaper to do very much of this kind of writing. And, second, many very good reporters are not writers of the caliber of Mailer, Wolfe, Capote and some of the others. Reporting generally is not much more than ten percent writing; it is about ninety percent headwork and legwork. One can be a very good, even an outstanding reporter, and not be an outstanding writer. But when a great writer puts his talents to journalism, you are bound to have a different form of journalism.

Michael Arlen, writing in *Atlantic*, says that the New Journalists are more "impresarios" than journalists. Tom Wolfe for example "presents Phil Spector," Jack Newfield "presents Nelson Rockefeller," and so on. And, of course, a good deal of their fame derives from persons they have covered or the kinds of people they have covered rather than from their work as standard journalists.

Harold Hayes, editor of *Esquire*, who had a lot to do with promoting and developing the New Journalism, calls it simply "literary journalism."

Dan Wakefield, a very fine reporter, became dissatisfied with traditional journalism and took to what he called "personal journalism." His book, *Between the Lines*, is an excellent example. At the same time Mailer's *Armies of the Night* came out in *Harper's*, Wakefield's piece called "Super Nation at Peace and

War" appeared in *Atlantic*. It was a marvelous piece, too; but Wakefield is not the powerful, overwhelming kind of writer that Mailer is. As a result, Wakefield came off second best. The timing was bad, to say the least.

Ray Boston, a colleague in the University of Illinois' Department of Journalism, formerly of the London *Times* and Reuters, the *Daily Mirror* and BBC, has an interesting view of the New Journalism. Boston stands in the literary, scholarly tradition of British journalism. (They have their sensationalist tradition also.) But being an MA from Oxford, and being trained in history, literature and philosophy, he has still another view of the New Journalism. He says that New Journalism is essentially comparable to "amateur" journalism, what was called "higher journalism" in England in the 19th century, when intellectuals went into journalism. It may be hard to think of someone like William Bagehot as an amateur; but, of course, he was—at least as a journalist. He was trained as an economist. His father was a banker and, indeed, he was born in a bank, because his father was so tied to the business that he made his home in the bank. He was the foremost authority on economics in his time. He took to journalism to spread his views about economics and to counter what at that time were traditional views on economics. During the period in question here, there were a large number of excellent periodicals developed in England. Out of this came a journalism that was engaged in mainly by amateurs as opposed to the professional journalist, who would do what he had to do or what he was assigned to do. While it might not interest him, or he might not always like it, he would do it. He might enterprise a story, but for the most part he did what he had to do or what needed to be done. The amateur journalist, on the other hand, was more inclined— indeed his basic motivation was and is today—to get himself before the public or his views before the public.

George Orwell was, in this sense, an "amateur" journalist, although today he is widely regarded as one of the very best in the history of journalism. This is to say that he was a self-directed "writer" doing what was accepted as journalism, not a "pro" doing whatever came his way or appeared on the assignment sheet.

He himself explains how he went about it in his *The Road to Wigan Pier*, now regarded as a classic in journalism.

> But I knew nothing about working-class conditions. I had read the unemployment figures but I had no notion of what they implied. . . . tramps, beggars, criminals, prostitutes . . . , and these were the people with whom I wanted to get into contact. What I profoundly wanted, at that time was, to find some way of getting out of the respectable world altogether. I meditated upon it a great deal, I even planned parts of it in great detail; how one could sell everything, give everything away, change one's name and start out with no money and nothing but the clothes one stood up in. . . . I thought it over and decided what I would do. I would go suitably disguised to Limehouse and Whitechapel (in the East End of London) . . . and pal up with dock labourers, street hawkers, derelicts, . . . and then, when I felt that I knew the ropes well enough, I would go on the road myself. . . . At the start it was not easy. It meant masquerading and I have no talent for acting. . . . [Eventually] down there in the squalid . . . subworld of the tramp I had a feeling of release, of adventure, which seems absurd when I look back, but which was sufficiently vivid at the time.*

Still another "amateur" was Ortega y Gassett, Spanish philosopher, writer and critic. Few people apparently know that his famous *Revolt of the Masses* was originally written as a series of newspaper articles in *El Sol*, when Ortega was a radical Republican in Spain in the late twenties and early thirties.

In historical perspective, what can be said about the New Journalism with some confidence, it seems to me, are about five things. First, there is something "new" about the New Journalism in the sense that, historically, it is quite different from what we have been used to. We have been used to the tradition of objectivity, of unbiased factual reporting, with the emphasis primarily upon gathering information, the finding and exploiting of sources,

*George Orwell, *The Road to Wigan Pier*, Victor Gollancz, London, 1937, from pp. 181-185. Selection reprinted by permission of Harcourt Brace Jovanovich, Inc. which reprinted the book in 1972.

and less on the writing. We have not been much concerned about using a variety of techniques of writing. We have basically produced a conventional kind of journalistic style which every student learns when he goes to journalism school.

Second, the New Journalism has historical roots or antecedents; that is, it is tied to history in a way that someone like Tom Wolfe is not always willing publicly to acknowledge, but must know. The New Journalists didn't invent the techniques they use. Rather, they are tied to history and to a very long tradition; indeed, some of it goes back to the Greeks. For example, Gail Sheehy, who is regarded as a New Journalist and writes for *New York* magazine, wrote a piece called "Red Pants." It is a "composite." If is a story of a New York City prostitute called Red Pants, but it turns out that there is no such person as Red Pants. She is simply a composite character. This is a very old technique, going back at least two thousand years to the Greek, Theophrastus. It is, of course, a very effective way to present information or some insight into what it means to be a prostitute, although whether or not it is bona fide journalism is a question, particularly if you don't warn the reader ahead of time that it is not a real person, but a composite. However, despite such arguments, such writing is now widely accepted as "journalism."

Third, historically it is clearly tied to the sixties—to the turmoil, the rebellion, the counter-cultural movements of various kinds in the 1960's. If Tom Wolfe dates it from about 1963 in his own story of how it all began, and Dan Wakefield writes about it in 1967, and the first book published about it came out in 1970, then clearly it is a phenomenon of the sixties, even though its roots may go far back in history.

Fourth, the appearance and the function of the New Journalism in our own time, in the sixties, and now in the seventies, fits a historical pattern of appearance and re-appearance of different types of writing, different types of content, and different approaches to journalism that occur again and again in American history, as well as in the history of the British press. For example, one can say, using Emery's meaning of the term, that when Benjamin Day started the *New York Sun* in 1833 he was providing a

"new" kind of journalism. There certainly had not been anything quite like it before.

When the Civil War came along, there was a demand for unbiased factual reporting, and we had a "new" kind of journalism—one that people had not been used to. Up to that time, American journalism had been mostly partisan, had been "advocacy" journalism, to say the least. Besides that, in 1848 the Associated Press of New York was started, finally becoming a national organization, a co-op of newspapers called the Associated Press. It was not much interested in advocacy or partisanship. In 1907, Scripps started the United Press, and Hearst started the International News Service a couple of years later. During this period, the "objective" tradition became fully established. (Peter Arnett, incidentally, has told me the tradition of objective reporting, of unbiased factual reporting, of non-opinion reporting, non-comment reporting, is basically an American invention and is so regarded throughout the world. It is, he says, the "American" tradition of journalism as opposed to the traditions of other countries.)

Similarly, when we come to Pulitzer, we find still another "new" kind of journalism. And later, when Hearst entered the field in competition with Pulitzer, we have "Yellow Journalism," another "new" kind of journalism. Some say it was nothing more than a revival of what had happened after Day started the *New York Sun*. But, in another sense, it was a "new" journalism because news became a kind of product, a commodity to be produced. In short, the production of news became comparable to industrial production of almost any other kind.

Thus, we have a number of traditions which run through American journalism; for example, the partisan, the sensationalist, the personal, and the objective. Now we have the "literary" New Journalism, which some regard as not having been a part of American journalism before, even if it was a part of the British journalism in the 19th century. But, again, if one goes far enough back in American history, one finds that Ben Franklin created a "literary" New Journalism in his time. Journalism before Franklin was mainly commercial news. It was not the kind of literary journalism Franklin provided; but then, again, Ben Franklin was a "writer."

Finally, with respect to its historical place and significance, the New Journalism clearly has made us re-examine the tradition of objectivity, the basic "American" tradition of reporting. It is quite possible, of course, that the objective tradition within a few years will be even more fully entrenched, though perhaps somewhat modified. On the other hand, the New Journalism may make inroads of which we cannot now be aware. After all, if we say that it really began only in the sixties, it has existed scarcely a decade. And that makes it far too early to tell what its significance might be.

JAY JENSEN is head of the Department of Journalism of the College of Communications at the University of Illinois. Dr. Jensen has been a reporter and editor for several newspapers. Additionally he has held positions in broadcasting and public relations. He has contributed articles to numerous books and journals and is co-author of Mass Media and Modern Society.

Professor Jensen is a member of Phi Beta Kappa, Kappa Tau Alpha and Phi Kappa Phi. He received his Ph.D. degree at the University of Illinois in 1957.

Professor Jensen is widely known as one of the most thoughtful of scholars in the field of journalism and mass communication.

In this chapter he has considered the development of the New Journalism and its historical antecedents. Dr. Jensen finds that most of what we call the New Journalism does indeed have direct antecedents but that it can be called "new" in the sense that it is journalism of a different sort from that which we have been used to in the recent past. He considers that the importance of the New Journalism may be in forcing a re-examination of traditional journalism.

3

The Noonday Underground from The Pump House Gang

By Tom Wolfe

JUST KEEP STRAIGHT. Keep your desk straight, keep your Biros straight, keep your paper clips straight, keep your Scotch tape straight keep your nose straight keep your eyes straight keep your tie on straight keep your head on straight keep your wife on straight keep your life on straight and that is Leicester Square out there and that is a straight square and this a straight office, making straight money—hey!—

—Noses straight up there!

—Line up those noses there!—there—is—an—office boy here, Larry Lynch, a 15-year-old boy from the Brixton section of London, staring up at the straight line of human noses. Occasionally someone—what the hell is it with this kid? Here he is, 15 years old, and he is dressed better than any man in the office. He has on a checked suit with a double-breasted waistcoat with a stepcollar on it and the jacket coming in at the waist about like so, and lapels like this and vents like this and flaps about so and trousers that come down close here and then flare out here, and a custom-made shirt that comes up like . . . *so* at the neckband, little things very few people would even know about, least of all these poor straight noses up here who make four times his pay and they never had a suit in their lives that wasn't off the peg. He is a working-class boy, and like most working-class boys he left school at 15, before the "O" level examinations. But he has been having his suits custom-made since he was 12 at a place called Jackson's. He has his hair regularly cut in a College Boy by a hairdresser named Andy. All—those—straight—

—noses up there have better jobs than he does, better addresses, they are nice old dads with manicured gardens out back and Austin 1100's, they have better accents, but he has . . . *The Life* . . . and a secret place he goes at lunchtime—

—a noonday underground.

Braaang—it is lunchtime. Why try to explain it to the straight noses? Larry Lynch puts this very straight look on his face, like a zombie mask, as if he were going to do the usual, go out and eat a good straight London lunch. All the straight human mummy-hubbies file on out for the standard London office-worker lunch. Boy! Off to the pubs to slop down the jowls with bitter and sandwiches with watercress stems in them. Or to Somebody's Chop House or Trattoria for the Big Time lunch, basting the big noonday belly and the big noonday ego with Scotch salmon, French wine and coq au vin. Or a Small Time lunch in some place that looks like a Le Corbusier cathedral with white grotto plaster and jazz-organ stained glass, serving nice steaming hot sliced garden hose on buns. But—Larry—Lynch—

—with—his—straight mask on walks over to Shaftesbury Avenue and then almost to Tottenham Court Road, in the heart of the Oxford Street shopping district. The sun—the sun is out today—the sun shines off the glistening flaws on thousands of bursting lonely beetled faces on the sidewalk at noon, but Larry Lynch cuts in the doorway at 79 Oxford Street, a place called Tiles.

It is like suddenly turning off the light. The entryway is black, the stairs going down are black, black walls, black ceilings, winding around and around, like a maze, down into the blackness, until there is no daytime and no direction and suddenly—

—underground at noon—

—a vast black room heaving with music and human bodies. Up at one end is a small lighted bandstand. There is somebody up there at a big record turntable and rock music fills up the room like heavy water—

Bay-beh-eh

—and in the gloaming there are about 250 boys and girls, in sexy kaks, you know, boys in codpiece pants, the age of codpiece pants, mini-skirts, mesh stockings, half-bras, tailored mons veneris, Cardin coats, navel-deep buttondowns, Victoria shoes, inverted pleats, major hair, major eyes—eyes!—eyes painted up to here and down to there, with silver and gold beads just set in there like Christmas balls, set in the false eyelashes—all of them bucking about, doing the Spasm, the Hump, the Marcel, the Two-backed Beast in the blackness while a stray light from somewhere explodes on somebody's beaded eyelashes—

—down in the cellar at noon. Two hundred and fifty office boys, office girls, department store clerks, messengers, members of London's vast child work-force of teenagers who leave school at 15, pour down into this cellar, Tiles, in the middle of the day for a break . . . back into *The Life*. The man on the stage playing the records is Clem Dalton, a disc jockey. Off to one side in the dimness is a soft-drink stand, a beauty parlor called Face Place and an arcade of boutiques, a Ravel shoe store, a record shop, a couple of other places, all known as Tiles Street. There is a sign out there in the arcade that says Tiles Street, W1. The place is set up as an underground city for The Life.

Right away the music is all over you like a Vibro-Massage— and—Larry Lynch just starts waffling out onto the floor by himself—so what?—who needs a partner?—a lot of boys and girls come here at lunchtime and go into this kinetic trance, dancing by themselves, just letting the music grab them and mess up their minds. Berry Slee, a 19-year-old fellow from Brixton, is out there, in the darkness at noon, heh, going like a maniac, doing a dance called Rudy, by himself, with this maniacal suit on, with flaps on the pockets hanging down about eight inches, messes your mind right up, and Berry's friend, Ian Holton, who is also 19, is dancing by himself, too, and god, this *green* suit he has on, it *messes your mind up*, this waistcoat with the six buttons grouped in groups of two, great green groupy work by the great Jackson, like, one means, you know, the girls are all down here, too, but so what, the point is not making it with girls, there are plenty of girls out here dancing by themselves, too, the point is simply immersing yourself for one hour in The Life, every lunch hour.

Linda McCarthy from the Ravel store is out here, dancing with some guy, ratcheting her hips about in their sockets. Linda, with . . . The Eyes, is about to make it, as a model or something, it could happen, but just now she is 17 and she works in the Ravel shop and one moment she sells a pair of jesuschristyellow shoes and then the music gets her like a Vibro-Massage and she leaves the store and she goes out there and dances it out and then comes back, to the store, sell-a-shoe, and Jane Dejong is out there doing that, god, maniacal thigh-swivel dance she does. One knows? And Liz White and Jasmyn Hardwick, Chris Gray, John Atkinson, Jay Langford, a 15-year-old American kid, from Los Angeles, only he is really English now, from Willesden, and Steve Bashor, who lives down on the Strand, and is 17 but looks about 21, and he has already been to sea, in the Merchant Navy, and come back and now every day, in the dark, at noon, he comes down into Tiles and stands on the edge of the bandstand and watches, he doesn't dance, he just watches and lets . . . the whole thing just take hold of him like the great god Vibro-Massage, and Sunshine Newman—oh god, Sunshine lost his job in the stationer's on Wardour Street but who gives a damn about that and Sunshine is going wild with some kind of yellow goggles on and his white turnover-neck jersey on, a checked jacket, sexy kaks. Who—cares—about the—sack—in—

—the—Noonday—Underground. Tiles has the usual "beat club" sessions on at night, with name groups up on the bandstand, and it packs them in, like a lot of other places, the Marquee, the Flamingo, the Ramjam, the Locarno Ballroom and so forth. But it is the lunchtime scene at Tiles, the noonday underground, that is the perfect microcosm of The Life of working-class teenagers in England.

The thing is, The Life—the "mod" style of life that got going about 1960—has changed within the last year. It has become a life of total—well, these kids have found a way to drop out almost totally from the conventional class-job system into a world they control. Practically all of them leave school at 15, so why do that old-style thing? Why live at home until you are 20 or 21, putting up with it all, having your manic sprees only on the weekends, having Mod and Rocker set-tos in the springtime or just messing up your mind on Saturday night at some dance hall.

Over the past year thousands of these working-class mods have begun moving away from home at 16, 17, or 18, even girls, girls especially, in fact, and into flats in London. They go to work, in offices, shops ,department stores, for £8 to £10 a week, but that is enough to get them into The Life. They share flats, three, four, five girls to a flat, in areas like Leicester Square—jaysus, *Leicester Square*—Charing Cross, Charlotte Street, or they live with their boyfriends, or everyone drifts from place to place. Anyway, it all goes on within a very set style of life, based largely on clothes, music, hairdos and a . . . super-cool outlook on the world.

It is the style of life that makes them unique, not money, power, position, talent, intelligence. So like most people who base their lives on style, they are rather gloriously unaffected cynics about everything else. They have far less nationalistic spirit, for example, than the orthodox English left-wing intellectual. They simply accept England as a country on the way down, and who gives a damn, and America as a country with the power, money, and if you can get some, fine, and the music is good, and you can get that, and they couldn't care less about Vietnam, war, the Bomb, and all that, except that English Army uniforms are indescribably creepy.

Their clothes have come to symbolize their independence from the old idea of a life based on a succession of jobs. The hell with that. There is hardly a kid in all of England who harbors any sincere hope of advancing himself in any very striking way by success at work. Englishmen at an early age begin to sense that the fix is in, and all that work does is keep you afloat at the place you were born into. So working-class teenagers, they are just dropping out of the goddam system, out of the job system, and into roles, as . . . Knights of the Codpiece Pants and Molls of the Mini Mons . . . The Life.

And nobody is even lapsing into the old pub system either, that business where you work your gourds off all day and then sink into the foamy quicksand of the freaking public house at night, loading up your jowls and the saggy tissues of your body with the foaming ooze of it all. Hell, one thing working-class teenagers know is that for five shillings, there is no way you can get drunk in the pub, but for five shillings you can buy enough pills— "purple hearts," "depth bombs" and other lovelies of the pharmacological arts—or "hash" or marijuana—Oh crazy Cannabis!—to stay high for hours. Not that anybody is turning on at Tiles in the noonday underground, but among working-class teenagers generally, in The Life, even the highs are different. The hell with bitter, watercress and old Lardbelly telling you it's time.

All that money, sodden with oozing foam, can better go into clothes. Practically all working-class teenagers in The Life devote half their pay, four to five pounds, to clothes. Some just automatically hand it over to their tailor each week because they always have him making something. There is no more contest between "mod" and "rocker" styles. The mod style and style of life have won completely. Working-class boys who do not dress in current mod styles—and they require a lot of money and, usually, a tailor—are out of it. Just like—shortly after Larry Lynch goes out there onto the dance floor, down into Tiles comes a 17-year-old kid wearing a non-mod outfit, a boho outfit, actually, a pair of faded Levi's and a jacket cut like a short denim jacket, only made of suede, and with his hair long all around after the mode of the Rolling Stones, and he talks to a couple of girls on the edge of the dance floor and he comes away laughing and talking to some American who is down there.

"Do you know what she said to me?" he says. "She said, 'Sod off, Scruffy 'erbert.' They all go for a guy in a purple mohair suit. That's what they call me, 'Scruffy 'erbert.'"

"What's your name?"

"Sebastian."

He turns out to be Sebastian Keep, who works in London as a photographer's assistant but comes from a wealthy family in Hastings. He comes down into Tiles from time to time during his lunch hour to see Pat Cockell, who is 19 and runs the Ravel store in Tiles. Both of them are from Hastings and at one time or another attended public schools and the hell with all that, but on the other hand they illustrate the class split that persists, even in the world of London teenagers.

All the articles about "Swinging London" seem to assume that the class system is breaking down and all these great vital young proles from the East End are taking over and if you can get into Dolly's, Sibylla's, or David Bailey's studio you can see it happening. Actually, the whole "with-it," "switched-on" set of young Londoners—or the "New Boy Network," as it is called, as distinct from the Eton-Harrow "Old Boy Network"—is almost totally removed from the working-class mods. It is made up chiefly of bourgeois, occasionally better, but mainly bourgeois young men and women in the commercial crafts, photography, fashion, show business, advertising, journalism. Aside from the four Beatles themselves and, possibly two actors, Terence Stamp and Michael Caïne, and two photographers, David Bailey and Terence Donovan, there are no working-class boys in the New Boy Network.

The New Boys, including a few upper-class adventurers and voyeurs, have borrowed heavily from the working-class mods in their style of life, but in a self-conscious way. Sebastian Keep's occupation, photographer's assistant, and his style of dress, 1964 Rolling Stones, are okay in the New Boy world. The suede jacket—cut and piped to look like a cotton denim pattern—cost 25 guineas, and this kind of reverse twist, like lining a raincoat with sable, is appreciated by the New Boys, but to the mods—well, 25 guineas is a hell of a mohair suit at Jackson's, with the lapels cut like so, like a military tunic, you know? and—yes.

Only the New Boys, the bourgeois, turn up to buy clothes in London's male fashion center, King's Road, in Chelsea. Both, the New Boys and the Mods, turn up in Carnaby Street, but more often the mods browse Carnaby Street like some kind of show place, or ambience, and then go off and have clothes like that made somewhere else, where it is cheaper, even a big chain outfit like Burton's.

Browsing Carnaby Street! God, before there was Tiles, that was what Sunshine used to do every day at lunch. Sunshine, whose real name is Tony Newman, of Stamford Hill, Tottenham, and who used to be called Blossom—well, Sunshine tops Blossom anyway—Sunshine would cut out of the stationer's store with the straight lunch mask on and then head straight for Carnaby Street and then just walk up and down Carnaby Street's weird two blocks for an hour, past the Lord John, Male West One, the Tom Cat, men's boutiques with strange enormous blown-up photographs in the windows, of young men flying through the air with some kind of Batman jockstraps on and rock music pouring out the doors, and kids just like him, Sunshine, promenading up and down, and tourists, christ, hundreds of tourists coming in there to photograph each other in front of Male West One instead of Big Ben, and busloads of schoolgirls with their green blazers on and embroidered crests on the breast pocket, all come to see the incredible Carnaby Street, which turns out to be a very small street with shops and awnings and people standing around with cameras in their hands, and Sunshines, all the Sunshines of this world, trundling up and down for their whole lunch hour, not eating a goddamned thing, just immersing themselves in The Life.

That was before Tiles. On Saturday nights in Tiles there is an all-night session with kids stroked out from exhaustion on the steps at the far end of the arcade and then they revive and struggle upright again and jerk and buck a little in a comatose awakening and then they are awake and back out on the dance floor. It is like the Sisters in white dancing, by themselves, to the shout band at the funeral of Daddy Grace in Washington, D.C., going into that ecstatic kinetic trance, oh sweet Daddy, oh big bamboo, dancing until they dropped, and then they were dragged off to the side, prostrate, and they stayed that way until their heads started twitching and then they got up again, those mountains of devout fat got to writhing again.

On Whitsun weekend Tiles goes all day and all night and everybody gets a glimpse of the Total Life, the day when they can all really live completely, all day long, in a world of mod style, drenched in music, suited up, flipped out, whipped, flayed, afire, melded, living a role—Knights of the Codpiece Pants. Molls of the Mini Mons—rather than a job. The whole idea of working-class or this class or that class will be irrelevant, except that—

—oh god, if only you could somehow make money without leaving The Life at all, the way Clem Dalton does, being a DJ, playing the records at Tiles, coming on with some swift American-style talk, having these great *performers* hanging around all the time, like Lee Curtis who sings at these American clubs in Germany, and Lyn Wolseley, who used to be with the Beat Girls and is a great dancer and everything. A DJ! So all these boys want to be DJs and they will do anything for a break.

Like Sunshine—one of Sunshine's big fears is that he is going to get stuck on another job like the one at the stationer's where he has to wear a necktie, because the thing is, Sunshine has developed his own variation within the mod style, which depends on wearing turnover-neck jerseys with these great tailored jackets, well—you know—a *white* turnover-neck can look great, practically formal.

Anyway, Sunshine went to Kenny Everett, who used to run the noontime sessions at Tiles. Kenny is also a DJ, and Sunshine wanted to get a job as a DJ at Radio Caroline or Radio Luxembourg, one of the pirate stations. It would be great, Sunshine heading out from shore for the first day, up in the front of a small boat, with his head up and the wind glancing off his yellow goggles, and his turnover-neck jersey, a red one, perhaps, up high, and his hands in his pockets. So Kenny Everett told him to make a tape and he would see what he could do for him. He told him just to come on with some patter like he was introducing a record, just some light patter, movement, not regular gags or anything.

So Sunshine got hold of a tape recorder and then the day came when he got in his room and held up the microphone of the tape recorder and then he concentrated on—what the hell is it these DJs say?—where does all that stuff come from?—and he could hear the voices of the DJs in his mind, all that stuff they say, things like, "Now, baby, one for the kidney machine, I mean one coming your way for the kidney machine, all those guys and gals down at the North College of Art, they're having their contest to raise money for the kidney machine, and Elise Thredder, down there at the college, you know what you wrote me about Cilla Black, Elise, you said I said she said we said they said oh my head, my head is—zowee!—now listen, Elise, I dig her, I dig her, I dig that girl, I'm telling you that, I've told you that, I dig her, I dig her, and I dig all those police cadets, I mean it, and this one's for the kidney machine and the police cadets, coming your way, and I'm sorry, if anybody catches me with me hand in the shop window, remember, I played this one for the police cadets, and the kidney machine, and club members everywhere, bless their little hearts, their lih-uhl 'earts, and their lih-uhl livers and their lih-uhl kidneys, no, I'm serious, ladies and gentlemen, and friends . . . I'm serious about this kidney machine, these gals at North College of Art are undertaking a most commendable endeavor, endeavoring to commendabobble the undertaker, you might say, in behalf of all those wonderful people with the—no—I mean that —and we're nothing until we're put to the test on the mountainside, and here it is, Mr. Billy Walker, and . . . A *Little on the Lonely Side.*"

How do they do it! So Sunshine does it. But he plays it back and it doesn't come out right somehow, he doesn't know exactly why, so he hasn't given it to Kenny yet, but someday, one day—

—one day Sunshine, and everybody, must find a way to break through the way Linda has. Oh god, Clem Dalton is the idol of the boys, they all want to be DJs, but Linda, who works in the shoe store, is practically the idol of the girls. Linda is on the verge of making it, of breaking through, making a living totally within The Life, and she is only 17.

Linda is a girl from Grays, in Essex. She left school at 15, like most of her six brothers and sisters, but they stayed in Grays, mostly, at home, until they grew up, but Linda, it is not that she is a wild girl or anything, it is just that . . . The Life, she was in it before she knew it. She could dance, and the way she wore her clothes—Linda doesn't have a skirt any lower than 7-1/2 inches

38

above the knees, that is the truth, and these great bell-bottomed trousers, and her eyes, well, she paints on these incredible eyes, a big band of shadow, it looks an inch wide, between the upper lid and the eyebrows, then a black rim underneath and then she paints on eyelashes, paints them on, under her eyes, with these stripes reaching in picket rows down to her cheekbones, and her black bangs in front come down and just seem to be part of some incredible design ensemble with her eyes, it is all a pattern, a mask—anyway, Linda moved to London when she was 15, and she and three other girls moved into a flat on the motherless Leicester Square and pretty soon Linda was completely within The Life.

She took a job as a clerk, but it was, like—you know?—a total drag, and Linda started coming down to Tiles at noon, it was like a necessity, to get into The Life at midday before she flipped out in the flunky clerk world, and she was down there one day with her great face on, ratcheting her hips away, gone in the kinetic trance, and Pat Cockell saw her. He needed somebody, a girl, to come work in the Ravel shop in the arcade, somebody who would comprehend what all these working-class mod girls wanted when they came in. So he asked her.

Linda walked down the arcade and into the shop, and even in there, in through the door, she could hear the music from the bandstand. She could hear the music and the dance floor and all those kids would be about 50 feet away, that was all, and it would be like almost being in The Life all the time. So she took the job and pretty soon she would be selling a shoe and then nobody is in the shop for a moment, so Pat stays in there and she goes out to the dance floor and gets into the kinetic trance for one number and then comes back and sells some girl a jesuschristyellow pair of shoes.

Linda was making £9 10s a week. About 25 shillings went to taxes, £2 as her share of the flat, £3 or £4 a week to clothes, at places like Biba—and 30 shillings a week for food. That's all! Thirty shillings—but god, look, she looks great, and what are all these regular straight three-a-day *food injections* for, anyway. And then one day Linda was selling a pair of jesuschristyellow shoes or something and then ratcheting about on the Tiles dance floor and somebody told Marjorie Proops, the columnist, about her, and she ran her picture and then Desilu Productions, the TV company, was doing something about London and they put her in a scene, and now these photographers come by and take her picture—and Linda is *on the verge*, she could become a model or . . . a *figure*, a celebrity, however these things happen, with Pat Cockell as her manager, oh god, Linda could make it, living The Life totally . . . and yet Linda doesn't really give all that much of a damn about it.

People come in and talk to Linda, like this American who was in there, and she listens and she answers questions, but then Clem Dalton puts on something out there, like *Hideaway*—

Hideaway . . . Come on! . . . far from the light of day . . . Come on! . . . leaving the world behind.

—and Linda's eyes kind of glaze over and her legs, in the pinstripe bell-bottoms, start pumping and then she is out the door and out into the dark, at noon, in Tiles. *That's where we're gonna stay.* And so what if she doesn't make it. The Life is still there, it is still available for less than £10 a week, Clem Dalton will never forsake, Jackson will live forever, *I-love-you drops, I-miss-you drops,* and Ian Holton will be abroad in the streets of London with a green waistcoat on that messes your mind up, and Berry Slee and Jay, Liz, Jasmyn, Jane, all the Jays, Lizzes, Jasmyns, Janes of this world—and Larry Lynch—

Hideaway—Larry Lynch looks down at his wrist, beautiful the way that cuff just sort of wells out, white, out of the checked sleeve, a half inch of beautiful Brixton cuff, debouching, and christ, he is already twelve minutes over, and he heads back through the maze of Tiles, through the black, like unwinding himself, and up the black stairs—volt!—the sun hits him and nearly tears his eyes out, but the same bursting beetled faces are still bobbing and floating past on the sidewalks and the same shops, hacks, cops, the same Marks & Spencer . . . the same Leicester Square and—oh splendid!—he knew it would be this way, there, back in the office, even, even, straight, straight, the same rows of . . . straight noses, all pointing the same way, toward eternity, as if nothing had happened at all.

TOM WOLFE is, of course, one of the major figures of the New Journalism—as both practitioner and promoter. His work is primarily that of a literary journalist. He is usually not cause oriented in his writing. His viewpoint is often that of fascinated observer. Wolfe has been called an electric writer, an impressionistic writer, a sensory writer. There is a sense in his writing of an acutely aware presence.

Wolfe earned a BA degree at Washington and Lee University and a Ph.D. in American Studies from Yale University. He began his journalistic career with the Washington Post, then moved to the New York Herald Tribune. It was during his years with the Herald Tribune in the early and mid-1960's that Wolfe and a number of others began to sense the possibility of something new in journalism and began to develop it.

Wolfe has been quite active in recent years in the critical discussion of the New Journalism. He considers the New Journalism to be primarily what we have called literary journalism; and he sees it as perhaps supplanting the novel in literary significance. He has recently produced a book, The New Journalism, in which he argues this point.

In his article one sees a number of stylistic factors typical of both Wolfe's work and, to some extent, that of other literary journalists. There is, of course, Wolfe's impressionistic style. Additionally there is the great attention to detail, description and scene-setting common to many of these writers.

4 The Book as a Medium for Journalism

*From a
discussion with*
Gay Talese

I HAVE BEEN categorized by many as part of the New Journalism. Privately, I resent being labelled as part of any group of writers and I don't particularly like the term New Journalism. I am not one who claims it is new. I can only talk in terms of what it is that I do. And this is what I propose to do here.

What I do is report and what I am is a reporter. I take pride in the term, and I do not identify with Mark Twain or any novelist who as a non-fiction writer years ago or centuries ago did what we might think of as New Journalism today. The fact that people like myself and others like David Halberstam and Tom Wolfe, Jimmy Breslin, and Dick Schaap and some others have left newspaper work is not a great tragedy for journalism. We reach a stage, some of us who pride ourselves in being reporters, of not having the room to go into the subject as deeply as we wish. We graduate first from newspaper reporting to magazine reporting and then the book. This is what I did, starting with *The New York Times* magazine when I was still working for the daily paper. Lester Markel, who was then editor of the *Times* magazine, was a great editor and the pieces that I did for him back in the late 1950's and the early 1960's, allowed me to grow in ways I was not able to on the daily paper. But even the *Times* magazine in those days had a limitation of 2,500 words on a piece. I found that to be a bit limiting and I went to longer magazine pieces, principally for *Esquire,* and then to book writing which is what I am doing now. The book I am working on now is a study of sex in America. It is reporting on the private lives of people. It is done in the same way that I did the book on *The New York Times* and the book on the Mafia family. I write about people. I try to report through the personal experiences of the people.

I see the book as the form for journalism now only because it allows me to do some things I could not do in periodical journalism. And, of course, the book can be a contemporary thing because books can be produced very quickly today. It need not take nine or twelve months to produce a book. So the writer can be almost on top of the news even in a book. Jack Newfield, whom I admire, is an example of being on top of something in his latest book on populism. The thing that books do for a writer is allow him to take all the room he needs to justify the amount of reporting he did. There is no space limitation. Magazines do not afford that luxury in space now, and I know that in my last year on *The New York Times,* which was 1965, space was far more limiting than it had been in 1956 when I started writing for *The New York Times.* It was a matter of cost—the rising cost of the newsprint and the rising cost of labor as well. These and many other factors caused what would have been a 900 or 1,000 word story to be trimmed to 650 or 700 words when I left the paper in 1965. I don't believe you can deal seriously with any subject in that amount of space if you do the leg work. If you write off the top of your head or do essays, which I did not, that is another matter.

There is a way for the newspapers to deal with the limiting amount of space available. Instead of having the reporter cover stories everyday, give him five or six days to do the research on a particular subject and then let him rewrite it a great many times to tighten the writing. There are not many journalists who are tight writers. They are not careful writers and they do not rewrite very much. In the nine years that I worked for *The New York Times* as a staff writer, I never wrote one paragraph the first time and got it right. I never wrote a lead that I did not re-write five or ten times even when I was on a rewrite. There was time. Many of the reporters who were colleagues in those days took pride in the fact that they were fast writers. We used to know certain people who were very quick and they could turn out a story in nine, ten or twenty minutes. I don't believe anyone should have revelled in that, although some did. I like to rewrite. Rarely am I satisfied with what I do finally, but it is a matter of doing the best you can, stealing all the time you can from the editor and the publisher. I never got a story in more than five minutes before the absolute deadline. Even if I started at two o'clock in the afternoon and the deadline was 6:30, I wouldn't get it in until about 6:25. I didn't see any reason why they should have the benefit of the time. I stole all the time I could.

The techniques I use in producing a book are essentially those of a good journalist. First of all, I pride myself in accuracy. I would put my accuracy in the books that I have done, the report-ing that I did in magazine form or in newspaper form with the ac-curacy of any of those that I admire and some that I don't particu-larly admire. I take time with my reporting. I write very slowly and check as much as I can on the accuracy of what I do. What I like to do is research. Research is the fun and writing is the pain in production.

In line with this emphasis on accuracy, I am often questioned about a technique that I, and maybe others, use in which I tell the reader what people are thinking and what people are feeling. I write that Lester Markel was thinking this or feeling this as he sat behind the desk on the Sunday Department of the *Times* on a particular occasion. How can I accurately tell what people are thinking? It is very simple. It seems much trickier than it is. In my recent reporting I have simply been trying to get away from di-rect quotations.

I suspect direct quotations. When I was on a daily paper, I found that it was not uncommon for reporters to change quotes within direct quotations. Since people did not speak in sentences or in paragraphs, since people in expressing themselves are not really very quotable—the reporter would often change a few words around, not necessarily alter the meaning, but just change the words. Sometimes there were three or four of us from different papers on the same story. I would notice the quotes I got weren't exactly the quotes that appeared in the *Herald Tribune* or the *New York Post*.

Also, I felt in daily reporting that reporters tended to get lazy in their writing. They would work hard on the first paragraph, a little bit less hard on the second paragraph and the third paragraph of the story would be a direct quote, almost formula writing. That's where the reporters would stop writing the story. They would ride the quotes down to a nine or ten paragraph story. I do not trust the direct quotations of people when a tape recorder is not used and I am much too lazy to carry a tape recorder. I also believe that I can be more accurate, capture more precisely what the individual that I am interviewing is trying to say, by taking what I know he is trying to say and what he is trying to convey. I can write it better than he can say it in most cases. I will use a direct quote when something is said in a unique way or particularly special way that an individual has.

Of course the interior monologue, at least the research necessary to produce it, is not possible in daily reporting. In *Honor Thy Father* and in the *Kingdom and the Power*, both books in which I used this technique, I interviewed people that were major figures some thirty, forty or fifty times. For example, in the *Kingdom and the Power* one of the major figures is the present managing editor of the *New York Times*, A. M. Rosenthal. I had fifty interviews with him. I got to know Rosenthal and others on the *Times* well not only from interviewing but from my previous familiarity with them since I worked for them and under them and around them. I knew from interviews and from my own experiences with them their attitudes, but I would not quote them directly. Instead of writing that so and so said such and such, I wrote they thought or felt it. And my sources were plainly those that I was writing about.

I also find that with this technique you can maintain your own writing style. You can give a kind of tone to your writing if you don't allow it to be broken into by a direct quote; you can bring your own style to your reporting. Simply take what a person believes or an attitude that he conveys to you or that you understand to be truly reflective of his attitude. Put it in your own words. It captures more accurately what that person is trying to communicate to you.

Of course, I do not get away from direct quotations when I am writing scenes that involve dialogue. When you get to know your subjects very, very well, and it is necessary to do that to do the kind of reporting in depth that I want to do, you find them in situations, or, in fact, wait for situations to occur, which provide interaction between the people that you are writing about. It happened in the *Kingdom and the Power*, in those scenes in the managing editor's office involving Clifton Daniel and Turner Catledge, or in another instance in the publisher's office involving the present publisher Arthur Ochs Sulzberger and James Reston. Now in both cases those scenes involved dialogue—dialogue that I had to get from all the persons who were involved. I like dialogue because it is dramatic and often very revealing.

In a piece on Frank Sinatra, I showed him walking in a pool room and getting into a fight with a young man. It was a scene that almost could have been fiction. I like to suggest fiction in the reporting that I do, inviting, perhaps, a skepticism on the part of some readers who think I make it all up. But I like everything to be verifiable, and I am very careful. I do take notes and I get down all that I can.

Still, even though dialogue can be very dramatic in this way, I am skeptical of its use. We who went to schools of journalism were taught this technique of putting things in direct quotations. For example, in the *New Yorker's* old Talk of the Town pieces you would have some quotations which would go on paragraph after paragraph. I really doubt the situation often presented in those pieces—a reporter walking into some lower Manhattan fish market and meeting some marvelous character who might have operated a tugboat and the tugboat captain starts talking about life on the old East Side or the Hudson River piers. And the reporter from the *New Yorker* would go on, sometimes ten paragraphs in a row of direct quotation, paragraph after paragraph directly quoted with never the questions the reporter obviously had to ask to elicit those kind of comments. The paragraphs were so beautifully phrased. You had a tugboat captain or a Democratic political leader in Brooklyn talking like a professor at Columbia. I never believed these quotes. People always spoke a bit better than my own reporting experience would have me believe. There was too much polish to the quotes.

The themes for my books come to me much as the subjects for a newspaper reporter's articles might come to him—though there may be more of a connecting thread between the book themes. *Honor Thy Father* was suggested to me by a Mafia man's wife. Her name is Rosalie Bonnano. Her maiden name was Profaci. She is about thirty-six now. Three or four years ago, she was angry at her father-in-law, the Mafia leader Joseph Bonnano, because the father had tremendous influence over his son, her husband. She felt he had led the son into the Mafia or if he had not led him into the Mafia he kept him there, not discouraging the son. Rosalie had gone to Catholic convents as most of these girls did—daughters of Mafia leaders or people who married into Mafia families. One day she tried to explain to me the failings of her husband and her own irritation with her husband at that moment, and generally with the Mafia men who are part of her life. If you are a Mafia wife you have bodyguards in the house at all times, bodyguards who spend the night, snore on the sofas, keep your own children awake. She was a harrassed housewife during the time that I was doing research for the book. She said to me "honor thy father indeed, that's what messed my husband up,"—"honor thy father indeed, that's what put my husband where he is." I thought about it and then used it.

The Kingdom and the Power was suggested by an editor at *Esquire* named Robert Brown. He was then fiction editor. The first piece on the *Times* that I did for *Esquire* was not my idea either, but was suggested by the [former] editor of *Esquire*, Harold Hayes from North Carolina. He wanted me to do a piece on the former managing editor of *The New York Times*, Clifton Daniel, who is also from North Carolina. I did that piece and it was during the writing of it that I got the idea of writing about

The New York Times as an organization. When the piece appeared in *Esquire*, it was called the "Kingdom and the Power and the Glory of the New York Times."

The book I am currently working on is, in one sense at least, about sex in America. I am getting the information for this book from two basic sources. First, from the so-called experts in this field, everyone from Masters and Johnson to Hugh Hefner to the famous Al Goldstein, editor of *Screw*, to marriage counselors, sexual therapists, leaders of nudist movements and other experts or self-proclaimed experts. But the reporting that I truly want to do and hope to do in this book will be about the lives of people who are not part of this "sex industry." I am interested in how people are living now and I'm interested in what I will be able to do in reporting private lives. Also I want to report fantasy. I am fascinated by fantasy. I would like to report on sexual fantasy. This of course will have to come from knowing the people terribly well and getting them to reveal as best they can what it is they use as fantasy.

The theme which runs through most of my writing, my book reporting, is the family. This is found not only in the *Kingdom and the Power* and *Honor Thy Father* but in another book that I wrote called *The Bridge*. I am interested in families, in how families are changing. This book about sex in America is really about the family in America. I am trying to do it in terms of the sexual change in family life. I am concerned and fascinated with change in family structure. No doubt this comes out of my own past. I come from a very strong family and I think it has helped me and has hindered me in certain ways too. Reporters who take reporting very seriously and who believe it can be an art form, bring much of their past to whatever it is they choose to report or to devote much of their time to as in a book length project. The family is one of the things I have written a great deal about, and probably will stay with.

One would like to think that such a great amount of time, the effort put into a book, the emphasis on careful writing and accurate research pays off. But I don't think it does as often as we would like to believe. There is too much junk that is selling these days. And this brings me to the point I made at the outset. If in the New Journalism we are dealing with people who bring the best of the so-called old journalism, which is legwork, to their work— people who do all the chasing around and collecting of information and then take the time to write it well—if those are elements which are brought to the New Journalism, then I would like to be identified with it. I believe, contrary to the criticism that Tom Wolfe has received from many people, that he is a hell of a good reporter. Wolfe is a man who has this electric style, a marvelous pyrotechnic style, this use of language which is very original, but he also does his homework. Generally he is a very careful, accurate reporter who brought a journalistic background to his own care in writing and his own particular rare style. I like to think that I and others do that. We are using the fundamentals of journalism and bringing into the writing something new—if indeed it is new.

GAY TALESE and Tom Wolfe are the two writers perhaps most frequently called New Journalists. Unlike Wolfe, Talese dislikes the term and frequently disavows it as a label to be attached to him. Talese's position is that he is a reporter. He says he has simply chosen the book as the medium for his journalism. He feels it allows him the depth he needs to treat his subject as he wishes. Similarly the style of writing allows him to tell the story as he wishes.

Talese is a graduate of the University of Alabama. He spent 10 years as a reporter with The New York Times. He has written extensively for magazines, especially Esquire. His best-known book-length works are The Kingdom and the Power, a study of The New York Times, and Honor Thy Father, a study of a Mafia family.

The following selection is from Honor Thy Father. The book deals primarily with the Bonanno family, a prominent Mafia family. In this selection Bill Bonanno is hiding with another Mafia man in an apartment during a very tense period. But as with much of Talese's writing we quickly slip from this scene to another time and place. There is a fluidity to Talese's writing. He so easily moves about in time and place. Another mark of Talese's writing, seen in this selection, is an absence of direct quotes. Instead, Talese tells the reader what his subject is thinking or feeling—much as a novelist might, a technique for which he is often criticized. Also, again note the emphasis on detail, common to many of the New Journalists.

5 | Selection from Honor Thy Father

By Gay Talese

BILL BONANNO, a tall, heavy, dark-haired man of thirty-one whose crew cut and button-down shirt suggested the college student that he had been in the 1950s but whose moustache had been grown recently to help conceal his identity, sat in a sparsely furnished apartment in Queens listening intently as the telephone rang. But he did not answer it.

It rang three times, stopped, rang again and stopped, rang a few more times and stopped. It was Labruzzo's code. He was in a telephone booth signaling that he was on his way back to the apartment. On arriving at the apartment house, Labruzzo would repeat the signal on the downstairs doorbell and the younger Bonanno would then wait, gun in hand, looking through the peephole to be sure that it was Labruzzo getting out of the elevator. The furnished apartment the two men shared was on the top floor of a brick building in a middle-class neighborhood, and since their apartment door was at the end of the hall they could observe everyone who came and went from the single self-service elevator.

Such precautions were being taken not only by Bill Bonanno and Frank Labruzzo but by dozens of other members of the Joseph Bonanno organization who for the last few weeks had been hiding out in similar buildings in Queens, Brooklyn, and the Bronx. It was a tense time for all of them. They knew that at any moment they could expect a confrontation with rival gangs trying to kill them or with government agents trying to arrest them and inter-rogate them about the rumors of violent plots and vendettas now circulating through the underworld. The government had recently concluded, largely from information obtained through wiretapping and electronic bugging devices, that even the top bosses in the Mafia were personally involved in this internal feud and that Joseph Bonanno, a powerful don for thirty years, was in the middle of the controversy. He was suspected by other dons of excessive ambition, of seeking to expand—at their expense and perhaps over their dead bodies—the influence that he already had in various parts of New York, Canada, and the Southwest. The recent elevation of his son, Bill, to the number three position in the Bonanno organization was also regarded with alarm and skepticism by a few leaders of other gangs as well as by some members of Bonanno's own gang of about 300 men in Brooklyn.

The younger Bonanno was considered something of an ec-centric in the underworld, a privileged product of prep schools and universities whose manner and methods, while not lacking in courage, conveyed some of the reckless spirit of a campus acti-vist. He seemed impatient with the system, unimpressed with the roundabout ways and Old World finesse that are part of Mafia tradition. He said what was on his mind, not altering his tone when addressing a mafioso of superior rank and not losing his sense of youthful conviction even when speaking the dated Sicilian dialect he had learned as a boy from his grandfather in Brooklyn. The fact that he was six feet two and weighed more than 200 pounds and that his posture was erect and his mind very quick added to the formidability of his presence and lent substance to his own high opinion of himself, which was that he was the equal or superior of every man with whom he was associating except for possibly one, his father. When in the

51

company of his father, Bill Bonanno seemed to lose some of his easy confidence and poise, becoming more quiet, hesitant, as if his father were severely testing his every word and thought. He seemed to exhibit toward his father a distance and formality, taking no more liberties than he would with a stranger. But he was also attentive to his father's needs and seemed to take great pleasure in pleasing him. It was obvious that he was awed by his father, and while he no doubt had feared him and perhaps still did, he also worshiped him.

During the last few weeks he had never been far from Joseph Bonanno's side, but last night, knowing that his father wished to dine alone with his lawyers and that he planned to spend the evening at Maloney's place, Bill Bonanno passed a quiet evening at the apartment with Labruzzo, watching television, reading the newspapers, and waiting for word. Without knowing exactly why, he was mildly on edge. Perhaps one reason was a story he had read in *The Daily News* reporting that life in the underworld was becoming increasingly perilous and claiming that the elder Bonanno had recently planned the murder of two rival dons, Carlo Gambino and Thomas (Three-Finger Brown) Lucchese, a scheme that supposedly failed because one of the triggermen had betrayed Bonanno and had tipped off one of the intended victims. Even if such a report were pure fabrication, based possibly on the FBI's wiretapping of low-level Mafia gossip, the younger Bonanno was concerned about the publicity given to it because he knew that it could intensify the suspicion which did exist among the various gangs that ran the rackets (which included numbers games, bookmaking, loan-sharking, prostitution, smuggling, and enforced protection). The publicity could also inspire the outcry of the politicians, provoke the more vigilant pursuit of the police, and result in more subpoenas from the courts.

The subpoena was dreaded in the underworld now more than before because of a new federal law requiring that a suspected criminal, if picked up for questioning, must either testify if given immunity by the court or face a sentence for contempt. This made it imperative for the men of the Mafia to remain inconspicuous if they wanted to avoid subpoenas every time there were newspaper headlines. The law also impeded the Mafia leaders' direction of their men in the street because their men, having to be very cautious and often detained by their caution and evasiveness, were not always where they were supposed to be at the appointed hour to do a job, and frequently they were unavailable to receive, at designated telephone booths at specific moments, prearranged calls from headquarters seeking a report on what had happened. In a secret society where precision was important, the new problem in communications was grating the already jangled nerves of many top mafiosi.

The Bonanno organization, more progressive than most partly because of the modern business methods introduced by the younger Bonanno, had solved its communications problem to a degree by its bell-code system and also by the use of a telephone answering service. It was perhaps the only gang in the Mafia with an answering service. The service was registered in the name of a fictitious Mr. Baxter, which was the younger Bonanno's code name, and it was attached to the home telephone of one member's maiden aunt who barely spoke English and was hard of hearing. Throughout the day various key men would call the service and identify themselves through agreed-upon aliases and would leave cryptic messages confirming their safety and the fact that business was progressing as usual. If a message contained the initials "IBM"—"suggest you buy more IBM"—it meant that Frank Labruzzo, who had once worked for IBM, was reporting. If the word "monk" was in a message, it identified another member of the organization, a man with a tonsured head who often concealed his identity in public under a friar's robe. Any reference to a "salesman" indicated the identity of one of the Bonanno captains who was a jewelry salesman on the side; and "flower" alluded to a gunman whose father in Sicily was a florist. A "Mr. Boyd" was a member whose mother was known to live on Boyd Street in Long Island, and reference to a "cigar" identified a certain lieutenant who was never without one. Joseph Bonanno was known on the answering service as "Mr. Shepherd."

One of the reasons that Frank Labruzzo had left the apartment that he shared with Bill Bonanno was to telephone the service from a neighborhood coin box and also to buy the early edition of the afternoon newspapers to see if there were any developments of special interest. As usual, Labruzzo was accompanied by the pet dog that shared their apartment. It had been Bill Bonanno who had suggested that all gang members in hiding keep dogs in their apartments, and while this had initially made it more difficult for the men to find rooms, since some landlords objected to pets, the men later agreed with Bonanno that a dog made them more alert to sounds outside their doors and also was a useful companion when going outside for a walk—a man with a dog aroused little suspicion in the street.

Bonanno and Labruzzo happened to like dogs, which was one of the many things that they had in common, and it contributed to their compatibility in the small apartment. Frank Labruzzo was a calm, easygoing, somewhat stocky man of fifty-three with glasses and graying dark hair; he was a senior officer in the Bonanno organization and also a member of the immediate family—Labruzzo's sister, Fay, was Joseph Bonanno's wife and Bill Bonanno's mother, and Labruzzo was close to the son in ways that the father was not. There was no strain or stress between these two, no competitiveness or problems of vanity and ego. Labruzzo, not terribly ambitious for himself, not driven like Joseph Bonanno or restless like the son, was content with his secondary position in the world, recognizing the world as a much larger place than either of the Bonannos seemed to think it was.

Labruzzo had attended college, and he had engaged in a number of occupations but had pursued none for very long. He had, in addition to working for IBM, operated a dry-goods store, sold insurance, and had been a mortician. Once he owned, in partnership with Joseph Bonanno, a funeral parlor in Brooklyn near the block of his birth in the center of a neighborhood where thousands of immigrant Sicilians had settled at the turn of the century. It was in this neighborhood that the elder Bonanno courted Fay Labruzzo, daughter of a prosperous butcher who manufactured wine during Prohibition. The butcher was proud to have Bonanno as a son-in-law even though the wedding date, in 1930, had to be postponed for thirteen months due to a gangland war involving hundreds of newly arrived Sicilians and Italians, including Bonanno, who were continuing the provincial discord transplanted to America but originating in the ancient mountain villages that they had abandoned in all but spirit. These men brought to the New World their old feuds and customs, their traditional friendships and fears and suspicions, and they not only consumed themselves with these things but they also influenced many of their children and sometimes their children's children—among the inheritors were such men as Frank Labruzzo and Bill Bonanno, who now, in the mid-1960s, in an age of space and rockets, were fighting a feudal war.

It seemed both absurd and remarkable to the two men that they had never escaped the insular ways of their parents' world, a subject that they had often discussed during their many hours of confinement, discussing it usually in tones of amusement and unconcern, although with regret at times, even bitterness. *Yes, we're in the wagon wheel business*, Bonanno had once sighed, and Labruzzo had agreed—they were modern men, lost in time, grinding old axes. This fact was particularly surprising in the case of Bill Bonanno: he left Brooklyn at an early age to attend boarding schools in Arizona, where he was reared outside the family, learned to ride horses and brand cattle, dated blonde girls whose fathers owned ranches; and later, as a student at the University of Arizona, he led a platoon of ROTC cadets across the football field before each game to help raise the American flag before the national anthem was played. That he could have suddenly shifted from this campus scene in the Southwest to the precarious world of his father in New York was due to a series of bizarre circumstances that were perhaps beyond his control, perhaps not. Certainly his marriage was a step in his father's direction, a marriage in 1956 to Rosalie Profaci, the pretty dark-eyed niece of Joseph Profaci, the millionaire importer who was also a member of the Mafia's national commission.

Bill Bonanno first met Rosalie Profaci when she was a young student attending a convent school in upstate New York with his sister. At that time he had a girl friend in Arizona, a casual American girl with a flair for freedom; while Rosalie was appealing, she also was demure and sheltered. That the young couple would meet again and again, during summer months and holidays, was largely due to their parents, who were very close and whose approval was bestowed in subtle but infectious ways whenever Rosalie and Bill would converse or merely sit near one another in crowded rooms. At one large family gathering months before the engagement, Joseph Bonanno, taking his twenty-year-old daughter Catherine aside, asked her privately what she thought of the likelihood that Bill would marry Rosalie. Catherine Bonanno, an independent-minded girl, thought for a moment, then said that while she was extremely fond of Rosalie personally she did not feel that Rosalie was right for Bill. Rosalie lacked the strength of character to accept him for what he was and might become, Catherine said, and she was about to say something else when, suddenly, she felt a hard slap across her face, and she fell back, stunned, confused, then burst into tears as she ran, never before having seen her father that enraged, his eyes fiery and fierce. Later he tried to comfort her, to apologize in his way, but she remained aloof for days although she understood as she had not before her father's desire for the marriage. It was a wish shared by Rosalie's father and uncle. And it would be fulfilled the following year, an event that Catherine Bonanno would regard as a marriage of fathers.

The wedding, on August 18, 1956, had been extraordinary. More than 3,000 guests had attended the reception at the Astor Hotel ballroom in New York following the church wedding in Brooklyn, and no expense was spared in embellishing the occasion. Leading orchestras were hired for the dancing, and the entertainment included the Four Lads and Tony Bennett. A truckload of champagne and wine was sent as a gift by a distributor in Brooklyn, and it was arranged through Pan American Airways to have thousands of daisies flown in from California because that flower, Rosalie's favorite, was then unavailable in New York. The guest list, in addition to the legitimate businessmen and politicians and priests, included all the top men of the underworld. Vito Genovese and Frank Costello were there, having requested and received inconspicuous tables against the wall. Albert Anastasia was there (it was the year before his murder in the barber-shop of the Park-Sheraton Hotel), and so was Joseph Barbara, whose barbecue party for nearly seventy mafiosi at his home in Apalachin, New York, three weeks after the murder, would be discovered by the police and would result in national publicity and endless investigations. Joseph Zerilli had come with his men from Detroit, and so had the Chicago delegation led by Sam Gian-cana and Tony Accardo. Stefano Magaddino, the portly old don from Buffalo, cousin of Joseph Bonanno, was given an honored ta-ble in front of the dais, and seated near him were other relatives or close friends of the Bonannos and Profacis. All of the twenty-four semi-independent organizations that formed the national syndicate were represented at the wedding, meaning that there were men from New England to New Mexico, and the group from Los Angeles alone totaled almost eighty.

Bill Bonanno, smiling next to his bride on the dais, toasting the guests and being toasted in turn, often wondered during the evening what the FBI would have done had it gotten its hands on the guest list. But there was little chance of that since the list, in code, had been in the careful custody of Frank Labruzzo and his men who were posted at the door to receive the guests and to es-cort them to their tables. There were no intruders on that night. There was not really a great deal of public concern over the Mafia in 1956. The Kefauver hearings of 1951 were already for-gotten, and the Apalachin fiasco was one year away. And so the wedding and reception proceeded smoothly and without incident, with Catherine Bonanno as the maid of honor; and Joseph Bo-nanno, elegant in his cutaway, presided over the gathering like a medieval duke, bowing toward his fellow dons, dancing with the women, courtly and proud.

After the reception, during which the bridal couple had re-ceived in gift envelopes about $100,000 in cash, Bill Bonanno and his bride flew to Europe for a honeymoon. They stayed for a few days at the Ritz Hotel in Paris, then at the Excelsior in Rome; they received special attention in each place and were ushered quickly through customs at the airport. Later they flew to Sicily, and as the plane slowly taxied toward the terminal building in

Palermo, Bill Bonanno noticed that a large crowd had gathered behind the gate and that a number of carabinieri were among them, standing very close to Bonanno's aging, bald-headed uncle, John Bonventre, who seemed rather grim and tense. Bonanno's first thought was that Bonventre, who had once served in the United States as an underboss in the Bonanno organization, was about to be deported from his native Sicily, to which he had gone the year before to retire, having taken with him from America a lifetime's supply of toilet paper, preferring it to the coarse brands produced in Sicily. After the plane stopped but before the door opened, a stewardess asked that Mr. and Mrs. Bonanno please identify themselves. Slowly, Bill Bonanno raised his hand. The stewardess then asked that the couple be the first to leave the plane.

Walking down the ramp into the hot Sicilian sun, mountains rising in the distance behind sloping villages of tan stone houses, Bonanno sensed the crowd staring at him, moving and murmuring as he got closer. The old women were dressed in black, the younger men had fixed dark expressions, children were milling everywhere, and the statuesque carabinieri, flamboyantly dressed and brandishing gleaming silver swords, stood taller than the rest. Then the uncle, Bonventre, bursting with a smile of recognition, ran with arms outstretched toward the bridal couple, and crowd followed, and suddenly the Bonannos were surrounded by clutching kissing strangers, and Rosalie, blushing, tried without success to conceal the awkwardness she felt in the center of swarming unrestrained affection. Her husband, however, seemed to enjoy it thoroughly, reaching out with his long arms to touch everyone that he could, leaning low to be embraced by the women and children, basking in the adoration and salutations of the crowd.

6 The "Truth" about Objectivity and the New Journalism

By Jack Newfield

THE NEW JOURNALISM does not really exist. It is a false category. There are only good writing and bad writing, smart ideas and dumb ideas, hard work and laziness.

Anyone who is less than thirty-five and owns a typewriter becomes known as a "new journalist." Writers as different as Jack Newfield, Eldridge Cleaver, and Rex Reed get lumped together under a contrived umbrella.

Everyone has his own definition of what the New Journalism is. It's the use of fictional techniques some say, or it's composite characterization; it's the art form that's replacing the novel, which is dying. Or it is anyone who used to write for the old *Herald Tribune* magazine; it's participation in the event by the writer; it's the transcendence of objectivity; it's anyone who makes up quotes; it's anyone who hangs out in the Lion's Head Bar.

To begin with, there is not that much that is new about the New Journalism. Personal advocacy preceded the who-what-when-where-why formula of the AP by a couple of centuries. Tom Paine and Voltaire were New Journalists. So was John Milton when he wrote his *Areopagitica* against government censorship in the 17th century. Objective journalism developed with the teletype and radio news.

Daniel Defoe, Stephen Crane and Mark Twain were all New Journalists according to most contemporary definitions. So was Karl Marx when he wrote for the *New York Tribune.*

Yet, something different and better does seem to have happened to mass publication journalism in the last fifiteen years. It is nothing more profound than a lot of good writers coming along at the same time, and a few wise editors like Dan Wolf at the *Vilage Voice* and William Shawn and Clay Felker giving these writers a lot of space and freedom to express a point of view.

But this rush of talent did not, as Tom Wolfe seems to suggest, spring Zeus-like from the *Herald Tribune's* city room in 1963. It appears, rather, the New Journalism crystallized at *Esquire* in the late 1950's furthered by economic competition with *Playboy's* sexist centerfolds, then attracting considerable advertising revenue away from *Esquire.*

It was during this period that *Esquire* published brilliant profiles of Joe DiMaggio, Frank Sinatra, and Joe Louis by Gay Talese. Talese managed to get inside his subject's private and interior lives, and give readers a deeper, truer sense of how things really are. At the same time Tom Morgan—now John Lindsay's press secretary—wrote equally rich portraits of Roy Cohn, David Susskind, and Sammy Davis, Jr. These are preserved in a book, called *Self Creations: 13 Impersonalities,* and some paperback publisher should wake up and re-issue it.

Then in 1960 an *Esquire* editor named Clay Felker had an idea, and assigned Norman Mailer to cover a real event—the Democratic national convention in Los Angeles. Mailer's piece was a masterwork of good writing and clear thinking. But it was not a new form. John Hersey, also a novelist, had written about a real event—Hiroshima. George Orwell had written about the Spanish Civil War. James Agee had written about the life of white tenant farmers in *Let Us Now Praise Famous Men.* So Mailer, who happened to be a novelist of distinction, wrote a remarkable work of journalism. And *Esquire,* in an economic war with *Playboy,* published all 30,000 words of it. Mailer opened a door with that piece, and the one he did on the Liston-Patterson fight. But it was not a new art form. He did not invent anything. He just wrote a great liberating prose. Just like Joe Mitchell, or A. J. Liebling. Or Westbrook Pegler or H. L. Mencken, or Lillian Ross.

I grew up on three journalists: Murray Kempton, Jimmy Cannon, and I. F. Stone. From Kempton I tried to learn irony and a sense of history; from sports writer Cannon, a love for the city and a sense of drama; from Izzy Stone, a reverence for facts, truth, and justice. Later, from Pete Hamill and Jimmy Breslin, I would learn the legitimacy of rage, the folly of politeness, and a sense of concreteness about the lives of ordinary people.

Then along came Tom Wolfe, with a history of the New Journalism in *New York* magazine that never mentions Kempton, Cannon, or Stone. Or A. J. Liebling or, Joe Mitchell, who wrote for the rival *New Yorker*. Like any faithful Boswell, Wolfe only mentions his friends.

What's called the New Journalism is really a dozen different styles of writing. Gay Talese and Truman Capote do one thing very well. Rex Reed has his own act. Breslin, Hamill and myself have certain things in common—a populist politics, working class backgrounds, respect for Mailer, Kempton, Cannon and a love for New York City.

And Tom Wolfe represents another strand in all this. He is a gifted writer, but he has the social conscience of an ant. His basic interest is the flow of fashion, in the tics and trinkets of the rich.

But if Wolfe represents a conservative approach, there is also the committed school of I. F. Stone, Mike Royko, David Halberstam, Tom Wicker, and many others.

Some alleged New Journalists like James Ridgeway are really part of an older muckraking tradition that stretches back to Lincoln Steffens and Ida Tarbell. So is Jack Anderson, who is considered an "old journalist" because he has a syndicated daily column.

Actually, the only really new journalism in America today probably is being done by people like Studs Terkel, Robert Coles and Paul Cowan who are trying to record history from the bottom, through the eyes of the average, unfamous people, rather than through presidents.

Wolfe wrote that the New Journalism "is causing panic, dethroning the novel as the number one literary genre, starting the first new direction in American literature in half a century." Nonsense.

First of all, there are still plenty of fine novelists around—Barth, Roth, Updike, Bellow, Ellison, Pynchon and Malamud are not living on welfare.

Second, some of the best "New Journalists" have found their own expanded form still so inhibiting they have turned to writing novels themselves—Hamill, Breslin, Joan Didion, Jeremy Larner, David Halberstam, and Joe McGinniss.

Third, most of us alleged New Journalists have read a lot of naturalistic fiction, and have been influenced by Theodore Dreiser, John Dos Passos, James Farrell, John Steinbeck, and Nelson Algren. This novelistic tradition seems out of fashion now, but what's called the New Journalism owes a lot of dues to it.

There is plenty of room for both good novels and good journalism. The need for newness, the competition of categories is just a game of egos. Why deny our roots? What is the need to claim historical novelty? What's wrong with giving credit to Jimmy Cannon and John Steinbeck, to Mencken and Steffens?

The distinction has also been blurred between what is called New Journalism and *underground* journalism. If New Journalism can at least be recognized by rich writing and lucid thinking, there is little of that in most of the underground press.

Most writers for most underground papers don't know how things really work, and lack the Breslin-Hamill instinct for the concrete. At this point, conventional "old journalists"—like David Broder, Jim Perry, Alan Otten, Martin Nolan, and Mary McGrory—write better and see clearer than the underground pundits.

The underground press has been very good at writing about certain things—the war, women's liberation, prisons, rock music. But it has been very bad reporting on other things—electoral politics, local government, crime and the fear of crime, and violence and arrogance when they happen to appear on the political left.

It was *Life* magazine that broke the Abe Fortas and San Diego scandals. It was Hamill's piece in *New York* magazine that first noticed the swelling rage in white workingmen's neighborhoods. It was the *Staten Island Advance* that first exposed the horror of Willowbrook Mental Hospital. It was Jack Anderson who exposed ITT. These are the sort of stories a better underground press might have dug out first.

Some press critics have tried to make "advocacy" the line that divides "biased, irresponsible" New Journalism from professional objective traditional journalism. But the most blatant advocacy journalists have always been on the right.

Joe Alsop advocated and predicted an American military victory in Vietnam for a decade. And Alsop helped Henry "Scoop" Jackson in his feeble campaign for the presidency as a participant. William F. Buckley might be the purest advocacy journalist in the whole country. He campaigned personally in New Hampshire for conservative Republican John Ashbrook. He is editor of a magazine with an ideological stance much more narrow and rigid than the *Village Voice*.

Somehow the concept of advocacy in journalism has become identified with the left. But what about the *Readers Digest?* They have published seventy-seven pieces on Vietnam since 1951, seventy-four of them in favor of the war. Does *U.S. News and World Report* present a balanced view of capitalism: Is the *Manchester Union Leader* fair and objective?

Objectivity can be defined as the way the mass media reported the history of the Vietnam war before the Pentagon Papers, the way racism in the North was covered before Watts; the way auto safety was reported before Ralph Nader. Objectivity is the media printing Nelson Rockefeller's lies about Attica until the facts came out that the state troopers had killed the hostages and not the inmates; that the troopers used outlawed dum dum bullets; that 350 inmates including some badly wounded were beaten after they gave up. Objectivity is printing a dozen stories about minor welfare frauds, but not a word about the My Lai massacre until Seymour Hersh. Objectivity is ignoring George McGovern as a joke until after he won the Wisconsin primary. Objectivity is believing people with power and printing their press releases. Objectivity is not shouting "liar" in a crowded country.

At bottom, I believe objectivity is a figleaf for covert prejudice. The point is not to equate objectivity with truth. It was objective to quote Joe McCarthy during the 1950's; it was the truth to report that most of what he had to say was unfounded slander. Today much of what Nixon, Humphrey and Rockefeller say are lies, but they are quoted without challenge, and given credibility.

The goal for all journalists should be to come as close to complex truth as humanly possible. But the truth does not always reside exactly in the middle. Truth is not the square root of two balanced quotes. I don't believe I should be "objective" about racism, or the tax loopholes for the rich, or the fact that parts of Brownsville look like Quang Tri. Certain facts are not morally neutral.

So, I think there is no such thing as a New Journalism. It still all comes down to good writing and hard work and clear thinking. The best motto for all of us is still the last line of James Baldwin's introduction to *Notes of a Native Son:*

"I want to be an honest man and a good writer."

Amen.

JACK NEWFIELD is a writer and editor for the Village Voice and is widely recognized as one of the abler practitioners of advocacy journalism. In his article, Newfield argues that traditional or "objective" journalism has often led to public deception rather than public enlightenment. Newfield says that the tradition of "objective" journalism causes the press to do little more than reprint the official line. Frequently the official line is a lie and the reporter knows it, but he can say nothing because "objectivity" has locked him in. Advocacy, on the other hand, can free him from such constraints.

The following article is an example of Newfield's advocacy. It is a reprint of an article by Newfield which appeared recently in the Voice. In the article Newfield discusses—attacks—a proposal for a new convention center in New York. Using facts, figures, the opinion of others and his personal, informed opinion, Newfield argues that the center will do great harm in the area in which it is to be built. The article was run by the Voice as a front page news story, not as a column of commentary on an editorial page.

In addition to Newfield's work with the Voice, he has written several books including A Prophetic Minority, Robert Kennedy: A Memoir and Bread and Roses Too. He is co-author of A Populist Manifesto. He attended Hunter College.

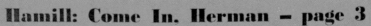

the village VOICE

15c

THE WEEKLY NEWSPAPER OF NEW YORK ● vol. XIV, No. 38 ● New York, N.Y. ● Thursday, July 3, 1969

Copyright © 1969, The Village Voice Inc.

IN FRONT OF THE STONEWALL

Photo: Fred W. McDarrah

GAY PROHIBITION CORUPT$ COP$ FEED$ MAFIA GRE

SOME GRAFFITI

'Gifted Offenders': I

Completing the Education Of the Black Ex-Convict

by Bell Gale Chevigny

In February, 1967, I was asked to teach an evening class in English composition at Queens College to a group of parolees. They were to be taught under the auspices of the state-supported program for the disadvantaged, SEEK  (an acronym for the rather fulsome Search for Education, Elevation, and Knowledge). Joseph Mulholland, director of SEEK, which was then half a year old, had been a probation officer and located the students through old associates on the parole board. There would be eight students in their 20s and 30s—all men, all but one black. I was teaching at Sarah Lawrence at the time, and the offer presented an irresistible contrast to my respect, quite apart from the extraordinary personal and educational challenge it held in itself.

But the challenge took on a shape I had hardly anticipated. The first evening we met I tried to find out where we stood by asking each in turn what he had enjoyed reading. Except for the two who began with magazines and worked their way up to "Marjorie Morningstar" and "The Fountainhead," they had done a good deal of reading in current black literature. Then, when it was his turn, a rangy young man, sprawling over his tiny chair and filling the space around him with expansive gestures, off-handedly listed all of Baldwin and LeRoi Jones, some Genet and Beckett—apologizing parenthetically for not understanding "Watt"—named Celine and Dahlberg, and paused. Before I could respond, a more compact and stationary figure across the room volunteered, "I've read most of that. And Hesse, I liked 'Steppenwolf' especially." The long man straightened slightly in his chair. "I forgot Gertrude Stein—she's the best." "Have you read 'Les Mots' by Sartre?" the other countered, adding softly. "That's 'The Words' in English." "Not yet," the first replied, keeping his cool, "but I read 'Nausea.'" "Nausea," 'Dirty Hands,' 'No Exit,' 'Being and Nothingness'—I guess I've read about everything of Sartre's," the quiet man

recounted. The long body remembered, the room snapped together, and whipped around to face him. "Incomprehensible?" he cried.

The soiled fellow replied wryly that he'd read them in the order in which he was able to get hold of them. His name was Arnold Kemp, and from that moment to began more or less to lead the class. (It turned out the only admirer of Gertrude Stein was not a parolee and had got into our section by mistake, but he stayed with us, expostulating, to the end.) When asked what he'd like to read, Kemp came up with out a fairly tale the likes of which the area has never seen.

father of the so-called black humorists.' When it came to the vote, although we'd talked about Camus, Faulkner, and Dostoevsky, one after another opted for "that Nathanael West." So dazzled was I that it wasn't until I got home that I realized that most of the class had taken West for a Negro.

It was like that all term. Whenever I tried to find out "where we stood," I risked being thrown off balance by sounding

Continued from page 12

View from Outside

Gay Power Comes To Sheridan Square

by Lucian Truscott IV

Sheridan Square this weekend looked like something from a William Burroughs novel as the sudden spectre of "gay power" erected its brazen head and spat out a fairy tale the likes of which the area has never seen.

The forces of faggotry, spurred by a Friday night raid on one of the city's largest, most popular, and tangiest fixed gay bars, the Stonewall Inn, rallied Saturday night in an unprecedented protest against the raid and continued Sunday night to assert presence, possibility, and pride until the early hours of Monday morning. "I'm a faggot, and I'm proud of it!," "Gay Power!," "I like boys!"—these and many other slogans were heard all three nights as the show of force by the city's

finest met the force of the city's finest. The result was a kind of liberation, as the gay brigade emerged from the bars, back rooms, and bedrooms of the Village and became street people.

Cops entered the Stonewall for the second time in a week just before midnight on Friday. It began in a small well-organized way. The plainclothesmen, two detectives, and two policewomen, were involved. But as the patrons trapped inside were released one by one around, started to gather on the street. It was initially a festive gathering, composed mostly of Stonewall boys who were waiting around for friends still inside or to see what was going to happen. Cheers would go up as favorites would emerge from the door, strike a pose, and swish by the detectives with a "Hello there, fella." The stars were in their element. Wrists were limp, hair was primped, and reactions to the applause were classic. "I gave them the gay power bit, and they loved it, girls," "Have you seen Maxine? Where is my wife—I told her not to go far," Suddenly the paddywagon arrived and the mood of the crowd changed. Three of the more blatant queens—in full drag—were loaded inside, along with the bartender and doorman, to a chorus of catcalls and boos from the crowd. A cry went up to push the paddywagon over, but it drove away before anything could happen. With the exit, the action waned momentarily. The next person to come out was a dyke, and she put up a struggle—from car to door to car again. It was at that

Continued on page 18

View from Inside

Full Moon Over The Stonewall

by Howard Smith

During the "gay power" riots at the Stonewall last Friday night I found myself on what seemed to me the wrong side of the blue line. Very scary. Very enlightening.

I had struck up a spontaneous relationship with Deputy Inspector Pine, who had marshalled the raid, and was following him closely, listening to all the little dialogues and plans and police deflections. Things were already pretty tense, the gay

customers freshly ejected from their hangout, prancing high and lesbians in the street, had been joined by quantities of Friday night tourists hawking around for Village-type excitement. The cops had considerable trouble arresting the few people they wanted to take in for further questioning. A strange mood was in the crowd—I noticed the full moon. Loud defiances mixed with skittish hilarity made for a more dangerous stage of protest; they

Continued on page 25

7 | Tisch Gang from The Village Voice *

By Jack Newfield

If you liked the Albany Mall and the World's Fair, then you'll love the new West Side Convention and Exhibition Center.

It will cost at least $200 million to build, and then will lose money. It is taking funds away from housing, schools, day care centers, and hospitals. It will open up another residential, working-class community to the real estate speculators. It will cause transportation chaos. It will cause a dangerous increase in air pollution by cars, buses, and taxis. (Former Air Resources Commissioner Robert Rickles told the Board of Estimate on May 3, "The effect of carbon monoxide on human beings is not a matter of conjecture . . . the operation of the Convention Center will kill people in Clinton.")

Despite all this, John Lindsay is pushing the convention center as if it were his personal monument to the city. "The Mayor wants this thing the way a child wants a toy," says State Senator Manfred Ohrenstein. "It's irrational."

The Planning Commission has already approved the center, and the Board of Estimate will vote on it on May 24.

*May 17, 1973; pp. 1, 103-105.

The guiding force behind this dubious boondoggle is real estate powerhouse Robert Tisch.

Tisch is a generous campaign contributor and effective fundraiser for Mayor Lindsay. He is also president of the Loews Corporation and president of the city Convention and Visitors Bureau. Soon after the state legislature created the public benefit corporation to build the convention center on March 2, 1971, the Mayor appointed his loyal friend Bob Tisch to be both president and chairman of the board of directors. The Mayor also appointed to the board of the public corporation another real estate developer, Seymour Durst.

The trouble is that both Tisch and Durst have tremendous real estate investments on the West Side, adjacent to the Clinton community. If the convention center is built, they will both profit personally. Tisch owns, through the Loews Corporation, a half-dozen midtown hotels, including the Howard Johnson Motor Lodge at 52nd Street and Eighth Avenue, the Ramada Inn at 48th and Eighth, the Summit at 51st and Lexington, and the Warwick Hotel at 54th and Sixth. Tisch recently leased the Americana Hotel to American Airlines.

The convention center will fill Tisch's hotels with businessmen and tourists. Since the public is paying for the convention center's construction, this amounts to an indirect subsidy to Tisch's private investments.

Durst is the most active midtown land assembler, owning several whole blocks in the area west of Eighth Avenue. (Durst also collects rent from four pornographic movie theatres on 42nd Street.) The convention center will likely double or triple the value of Durst's property on the West Side. It seems to have been a clear conflict-of-interest for the Mayor to have appointed Tisch and Durst to the board.

This is especially so because the Clinton community has proposed a practical, and probably superior alternative site for the convention center—the Penn Central railyards at 33rd to 37th Streets, Eleventh to Twelfth Avenues. The local planning board, the Clinton Planning Council; and every elected representative on the West Side has endorsed the alternate site.

The city, however, has refused to even consider the Penn Central site, a rigidity that becomes suspicious in the context of the Tisch and Durst real estate investments adjacent to Clinton. And their past campaign contributions to Lindsay. And Lindsay's possible need for future campaign funds.

When a critic of the center asked Lindsay why the administration had dismissed the Penn Central site so quickly, Lindsay said the real reason was that the condemnation costs of the alternative site would be "prohibitive." But when this skeptic called an executive of the bankrupt Penn Central, he was informed the city never even made an appraisal of the site.

Another apparent conflict of interest involves Comptroller Beame, although his conflict is legal and moral, rather than financial.

Beame is a member of the convention center's board of directors. But Beame will also have four votes on May 24 when the Board of Estimate votes on whether to approve the building of the center. Several lawyers believe it would violate the city's code of ethics for Beame to vote on the matter.

When it was suggested to a Beame campaign fund-raiser that the Comptroller disqualify himself from the May 24 vote, the fund-raiser replied: "The real estate guys would never let Abe do that. They own him."

For the last month I have been looking into the convention center project. Even most of its critics believe it is inevitable, that it's futile to expose it, that there is too much money and power behind it, that it has developed its own blind momentum. Nevertheless, I think there are at least three persuasive reasons the Board of Estimate should reject the convention center when it comes to a vote on May 24.

1) *The convention center will probably destroy Clinton as a distinctive, low-rent residential neighborhood.*

The center itself will not require any housing demolition; the plan is to build it along the river between 44th and 47th Streets. But the center will—and already has—attracted real estate speculators into the area. This hotel-luxury housing-motel development is inevitable, and will mean the end of Clinton as an authentic city neighborhood.

A community like Clinton is irreplaceable. It took a half a century to give it its special character, and once it is gone, it is gone forever.

It is neighborhoods like Clinton and Belmont and Williamsburg and Corona that make New York City what it is. A strong sense of community, of family, of religion, of immigrant culture is something planners and bureaucrats and developers can't quite comprehend as part of the soul of the city.

Bureaucrat-politicians Ken Patton and Alton Marshal are both on the board of directors of the convention center corporation. Both are elitist, upwardly mobile hustlers after power.

Marshal was the top man on Governor Rockefeller's staff in Albany, and now he is president of Rockefeller Center, and the chief spokesman for the nexus of banks, property, and capital the Rockefellers control. Ken Patton is Lindsay's Economic Development Administrator, and seems to be the villain behind the city's misguided effort to evict 37 mostly Polish families in the Northside section of Brooklyn, another stable, ethnic community.

Ambitious bureaucrats like Marshal and Patton don't seem to like, or understand, the sort of ordinary people who live on 3rd Street in Northside, or on Arthur Avenue in Belmont, or on Tenth Avenue in Clinton.

Last month *Voice* writer Judy Coburn interviewed Patton about the Northside evictions. "It's a matter of personal taste to live in a place like that," Patton said. "I don't like to live that way."

Now that John Lindsay is a lame duck, Patton is already hustling after the job of director of the Port Authority.

The Clinton neighborhood includes the West 40s and 50s, from Eighth Avenue to the Hudson River. It used to be all workingclass Irish and Italian. Now it's about 25 per cent Hispanic, but still predominantly Irish and Italian.

Most of the residents of Clinton were born and raised there. Apartments in the area rent for an average of $100 a month. The churches in the community, like Sacred Heart and Holy Cross, are crowded every Sunday; last Sunday morning the streets were filled with children dressed up for their first communion. About 30 per cent of the residents walk to work. Clinton boasts the city championship team in school yard roller hockey. It is precisely the sort of neighborhood the city should be doing everything possible to preserve.

But the real estate developers have been pushing the people out gradually over the years, just like in Chelsea and Yorkville. The population of Clinton was 54,113 in 1950. By 1960 the figure had dropped to 43,399. The 1970 census counted the neighborhood population at 35,657.

These families have been driven out of their homes by institutional expansion (mostly hospitals) and by real estate developers. Almost none have been relocated in the community; they have been pushed to New Jersey or Queens. Where they once lived, near Tenth and Eleventh Avenues, there are now motor inns, parking lots, gas stations, and luxury housing going up. The Clinton residents now feel they have no say in what happens to them, that remote, faceless planners decide what happens to their block.

In the past two years, since plans for the convention center were announced, the vulture-developers have stopped circling, and started pecking at the guts of the community.

On 49th Street and Eleventh Avenue, Sylvan Lawrence has bought a square block and will build luxury housing. Seymour Durst has sold a square block on 42nd Street, west of Ninth Avenue, to Richard Ravitch, and Ravitch will build two 45-story towers at $100 a room, meaning a family of four has to earn about $35,000 a year to live there. Jacob Fine has recently bought dozens of parcels in the area, and Jacob Fine is not a respectable developer like Ravitch. Fine is a notorious slumlord, whose home on Central Park West is often picketed by angry tenants. Fine now owns more than 100 separate plots of land in Clinton.

Irving Maidman, who owns a dozen porno properties in Times Square, has also been buying up parcels of land around Clinton; Maidman recently paid $250,000 in cash for four plots on West 47th Street.

The Glick Construction Corporation will build a high-rise at 42nd Street and Eleventh Avenue. On 57th Street, H. R. Shapiro, Inc., has started construction of a 48-story luxury apartment house, the Parc Vendome Tower. Shapiro got a special variance for the tower from the city; his lawyer was Bunny Lindenbaum.

The point is that all this real estate development is for the upper classes. It will gradually ruin the special working-class quality of Clinton; it will drive up rents; it will lead to more hotels and luxury high-rises and office buildings and motels. Eventually, when the convention center is open there will be honky-tonk bars, peep shows, and prostitutes—and the Clinton of churches and low-rent apartments will be a memory.

The one thing a government can't build or replace is a neighborhood. The luxury development is like a plastic glacier moving across the cityscape, killing the community life, and spreading impersonality.

Lindsay apparently thinks you save a city by building $200 million convention centers in Manhattan that attract business and tourists. But a city, as Jane Jacobs told us, is vital, diverse neighborhoods. And that is the thing Lindsay doesn't seem to appreciate. Lindsay has never actually lived in a neighborhood his whole adult life; he went from St Paul's to Yale, to the Navy, to Congress, to Gracie Mansion, without ever experiencing the special pleasures of place.

Of the 10 people on the board of directors for the convention center corporation, only one—William Sansone—actually lives in Clinton. He usually gets out-voted nine to one.

Impatient with Sansone's thoughtful objections, Tisch created an executive committee of the board of directors that excludes Sansone. This executive committee does not exist in the original legislation that created the center's public corporation.

2) *The financing for the convention center has become excessive, and its need has become doubtful.*

When the convention center was first announced, the public was told it would cost $100 million, and that money would come from a tax-exempt bond issue floated by the public benefit corpo-

72

ration. But the estimated cost rose to $140 million, and then to $200 million, and the bond issue could not be sold. So the corporation recently persuaded the city government to issue the bonds, and pay for the construction costs through the capital budget, at $50 million for each of the next four years.

If the center is built for $200 million, debt service on this expenditure would be more than $14 million a year. Based on recent experience with the Albany Mall and other projects, a good, skeptical guess is that the center will actually cost $300 million before it is completed. The most expensive public facility built in the last decade was Shea Stadium—and that only cost $26 million.

Moreover, a marketing study conducted by the Arthur D. Little Company *for the convention center corporation* projected "operating deficits totaling $915,000 for the first three years of operation (1976-79)."

The Little study anticipated a surplus in the fourth year, but premised this on a 68 per cent occupancy rate. But no equivalent trade show facility in any other city approaches a 68 per cent occupancy rate. The two most successful centers in the nation— McCormack Place in Chicago, and the New York Coliseum—both have less than 60 per cent occupancy rates. Last year the brand new McCormack Place had an operating deficit of $113,000. Cobo Hall in Detroit, with a 25 per cent occupancy rate, had a $500,000 deficit.

These statistics suggest the convention center could lose money indefinitely, and more importantly, perhaps there is no economic reason or need to build it at all. Many experts believe the existing combination of the Coliseum, Madison Square Garden, and the World Trade Center is sufficient.

There is also a question of priorities—whether the Lindsay administration should be spending $200 million for one facility that will benefit only a narrow economic interest in the city—the hotel and tourist industry in Manhattan. What about the rest of the city, the outer boroughs? Couldn't that money be more wisely spent on the larger interest of the city's population as a whole?

The $200 million in capital funds could be used to build housing and schools, for parks and day care centers, for police cars and sanitation trucks, for neighborhood health centers and air-conditioned subway cars.

These would seem to be more reasonable priorities for public funds than Bob Tisch's hotels.

3) *The convention center will cause a considerable environmental health hazard.*

There is no public transportation access to the convention center site. On some days 10,000 or 15,000 people will converge on the center by car, taxi, and bus. This will add a tremendous quantity of gasoline pollutants to the air, already filled with fumes and exhaust from the adjacent West Side Highway.

It is already official city policy to discourage citizens from driving their own cars into the midtown area, but the convention center is certain to inspire epic traffic congestion on the residential streets of Clinton. And it is this congestion that will poison the air with carbon monoxide, lead, and other unhealthy chemicals.

Robert Rickles, who helped defeat the 1971 transportation bond issue, spoke to the Board of Estimate on May 3 about the center's contribution to pollution:

"The operation of the convention center is in clear violation of the achievement of ambient air standards. Everywhere around the site, during the days of operation, standards for carbon monoxide will be violated. . . . If the facility produces traffic, which in turn creates violations of the Clean Air Act, the state or federal government may act to shut down the facility. That is the fate that awaits the convention center—expenditures of hundreds of millions of dollars and an empty hall.

"It will be empty because the operation of the convention center will kill people in Clinton. Our calculations indicate that concentrations of carbon monoxide on the streets of Clinton will be far in excess of federal standards. On the streets between 42nd and 50th, and on Eleventh Avenue, hourly averages will exceed 50 ppm and eight-hour averages will reach 20 ppm, as compared with federal levels of 35 ppm, and 9 ppm, respectively. Levels by the Twelfth Avenue underpass will reach 100 ppm. . . .

"There will also be a terrible impact upon the children of

74

Clinton, who, because of a lack of recreational facilities, must play on the streets. They will be exposed to lead from car exhausts. While carbon monoxide is most dangerous to males over 40, lead is dangerous to everyone."

The convention center is a polite swindle by a gang of con artists. It doesn't matter that this is a gang of millionaires who eat lunch at "21", contribute to worthy charities, and own Picassos. This bunch of developers is smart enough to disguise its greed behind a figleaf of boosterism and civic uplift.

New York City is obviously in trouble. There are more than a million citizens on welfare. A half million people are living in substandard housing. Brownsville looks like the moon. Fifteen-year-olds are pulling stick-ups to get money for heroin. People in the South Bronx are living in abandoned cars. To spend $200 million on a boondoggle like the convention center is almost demented.

It's up to the Board of Estimate to say no to the Tisch Gang. If they say yes, it will be the biggest real estate rip-off since the Dutch bought Manhattan Island for $24 worth of trinkets.

8 | Objective Journalism

By Lester Markel

LET US BEGIN with definitions. Strange words—objectivity and object. You can object to an object and assume you are objective about it, even though you may be only objectionable. The word objectivity suggests cold, calculated precision. It is not that simple. No human being can be totally objective; emotion has a way of intruding upon reason.

Please do not misunderstand, however. The ideal of objectivity, even though its full realization is humanly impossible, nevertheless must be kept always to the forefront. At least do not discard it right off and plump without reservation for personal or advocacy journalism—editorial, subjective journalism.

Before developing that point, more definitions may be useful—a definition of news especially. In the old days the saying was that if a dog bites a man it is not news but if a man bites a dog it is. That saying is wrong on two counts: if the man bitten happens to be Henry Kissinger or Richard Burton or if the dog that does the biting happens to be Lassie it is decidedly news—or, at any rate, a kind of news.

In any case, the old formula will not do in these days of complicated and cosmic happenings. News now must mean much

76

more than the factual coverage of spot events. It must include the broader trends, the recording and appraisal of the strong currents that run in the far-from-pacific ocean that is the world today. The kind of reports that sufficed in simpler days are no longer adequate to provide understanding. Interpretation is an essential element; without background the reader cannot arrive at any reasonable conclusions about such complex subjects as Vietnam, inflation, pollution.

There is a great hullabaloo in journalistic circles about this issue of interpretation. Some editors see in it great peril, others great promise. There are confusions, disagreements, little meeting of the minds; most of all, there is a failure to discern the difference between interpretation and opinion.

I see no reason for this difficulty. Interpretation is an objective judgment—as objective as human judgment can be—based on knowledge and appraisal of a situation. In addition to true information, it provides sound analysis, revealing the deeper sense of the news, providing setting, sequence and, above all, significance. Opinion, on the other hand, is subjective and personal.

Recognition of this distinction is of the utmost importance. Take a primitive example: (1) to report that Spiro Agnew attacks the press is news—or used to be; (2) to explain why Mr. Agnew makes the attack is interpretation; (3) to assert that Mr. Agnew is a rad-unlib and should be Spiro-ed is opinion (even though that opinion may be justified). One process is logical, while the other is emotional.

The opponents of interpretation insist that to insure "objectivity" the reporter must "stick to the facts"; if he attempts interpretation, they say, inevitably he moves into the area of opinion. But what "facts" are these editors talking about? The average reporter collects fifty facts and out of the fifty selects twelve as the important ones, leaving out thirty-eight. This is the first exercise of judgment. Then he decides which of the twelve facts should constitute the lead or first paragraph of the story; this fact gets prime attention because many readers do not go beyond the first paragraph. Second exercise of judgment. Then the news editor decides whether the story shall go on page 1 or on page 29; on page 1 it has considerable impact, on page 29 it may go unread. Third exercise of judgment.

Three judgments are involved in this so-called formula for "objectivity," for this "factual" reporting. Are the kind of decisions required for interpretation any different from the kind of judgments involved in the selection and the play of facts?

Interpretation is an essential part of the news. As for opinion, it should be confined to the editorial pages of newspapers and distinctly labeled on television and radio broadcasts. If there is to be crusading, let it be done by the knights of the editorial round table; let reporters seek other holy grails.

*　*　*

This issue of objectivity is involved also in the confrontation between the so-called New Journalists and those whom these current crusaders dub the "Ancient Order of Hibernators." It has become a paramount issue; it is discussed by panels on television; it is debated in seminars; it confuses almost everybody. It is a hot even if unenlightened debate. By some the New Journalism is likened to the dawn of an historic day in literature. By others it is compared to the onset of a plague of editorial locusts.

The New Journalism, according to its leading advocates, supplies a fresh and essential approach to reporting, making possible what they call "the revelation of the truth." The critics insist that the New Journalism is a spurious Baedeker, a phony map to editorial turnpikes; rather than providing directions to the truth it leads to credibility detours.

I have conducted fairly exhaustive research into the New Journalism. I have examined numerous dissertations and questioned some of the high priests of the order. I have read Truman Capote, who started it all with his *In Cold Blood*, which he anointed a "non-fiction novel"; talked with Clay Felker, editor of *New York* magazine, patron saint and one of the keepers of the "New Jay" aviary; with Tom Wolfe, the unofficial and very articulate secretary and scribe of the sect; and with Gay Talese, whose ardent devotion to the New Journalism is attested by his books—*The Kingdom and the Power*, in which he told all and more about what he pictured as the not-so-good, not-so-great *New*

York Times, and *Honor Thy Father,* in which he performed the same kind of hysterectomy on the Mafia.

The search for a definition of the New Journalism requires the combined talents of Diogenes, Sherlock Holmes and Clifford Irving. Wolfe remarks that the new creed requires "all three talents, reporting, analysis, and, above all, the dramatic techniques of fiction. . . . The 'New Journalism' involves a depth of reporting and an attention to the most minute facts and details most newspaper men have never dreamed of. To pull it off you casually have to stay with the people you are writing about for long stretches . . . days, weeks, even months."

Talese offers this: "The 'New Journalism,' though often reading like fiction, is not fiction. It . . . seeks a larger truth than is possible through the mere compilation of verifiable facts, the use of direct quotations, adherence to the rigid organizational style of the older form. . . . I attempt to absorb the whole scene . . . and then I try to write it all from the point of view of the persons I am writing about, even revealing whenever possible what these individuals are *thinking.*"

As an added starter there is Gloria Steinem, an editor of *Ms,* a formidable combination of Joan of Arc and Carrie Nation, who scorns the "who-when-where-what-why story"—a formula which "in inverted pyramid form is not one for writers, it's one for telegraph operators. You can only make sense of a situation by giving the human viewpoint, which is opinion."

*   *   *

The New Journalists appear to have little doubt about the validity of the concept. They seem to agree: that they are applying the "techniques of fiction" to non-fiction and providing "reporting in depth," "psychological insights," "meaningful dialogue," "truth not merely facts." (This involves, they explain, a deep and long process of inquiry, the kind of insight that "factual reporting" cannot achieve.)

Yet these conversations with leading New Journalists reveal differences over interpretation, procedure and even nomenclature. Some, the elite, do an intensive job of investigation; one might label them the "Diggers." Others do only casual and often careless research; one might call them the "Skimmers." The "Diggers" disavow the "Skimmers" as false preachers of the faith and polluters of the New Journalism stream. Unfortunately, there are more "Skimmers" than "Diggers."

There are also divergences among the New Journalists over definition and philosophy. Talese speaks favorably of the "New" in comparison with the "Old" journalism; Felker deplores the use of both terms. Talese talks of the "techniques of fiction." Wolfe concedes that maybe the word "fiction" should not be used and that, more accurately, the process should be described as one that employs "all the techniques known to prose." (He is wary, as understandably he should be, that the word "fiction" implies to the innocent bystander something that is "fictitious.")

But whatever the objections, certain practices of some of the New Journalists are disturbing—the portrayal of a composite rather than a single character (only thus, the New Journalists hold, can the profile be rounded and complete); the collapsing of a sequence of happenings over a considerable period into a single episode on a single day (only thus, they contend, can the typical event be portrayed); the reporting of talk that might or should have taken place, even if it didn't (only thus, they believe, can the subconscious be brought to the surface for the reader to behold); and, finally, a most casual regard for "facts." ("It is often possible," says David Freeman, "for facts to get in the way of real truth.")

* * *

Out of these observations, three definite conclusions emerge: first, that the New Journalism is really not new; second, that only in the broadest sense is it journalism; and third, that many of the New Journalists fail to recognize that the "New" is not a substitute for the "Old" journalism and that journalism generally has been in process of change.

As for the newness of the concept, surely reporting in detail and in depth reaches far back in literature. Boswell's accounts of Dr. Johnson's doings would certainly qualify as New Journalism. And there are countless other examples.

Consider then the word "journalism." It is derived from the

French "journal" (daily), which in turn stems from the Latin "diurnal," the adjective for "dies" (day). In the strict sense, it does not contemplate reporting and writing "for long stretches—days, weeks, even months"; it is concerned with the happenings of the day, with the news. Those who practice reporting in depth for weeklies and monthlies as well as dailies are journalists. But the New Journalists should more properly be called "factual fictionists" or possibly "deep-see reporters" rather than journalists.

Now, about the so-called "Old" journalism. The New Journalists contemptuously tag it as the "who-what-when-where-how-and-why school." So one asks: is it not the job of the news-gatherer and the news-purveyor to answer these questions with as much insight as he can? Are the facts to be ignored? How do the New Journalists propose to cover, for the same or the next day's newspaper, stories such as the admission of China to the United Nations, or Phase III of the Big Freeze, or an Attica outbreak or the shooting of a Kennedy?

Of the twelve to fourteen articles on the first page of the average newspaper, at least ten cannot be covered in the minute detail or with the dialogue and the colorful sidelights which the New Journalists prescribe. There is simply not the time to do this kind of job, desirable as it may be, unless the newspaper is willing to yield the news field entirely to television.

Furthermore, the New Journalists depend in large degree on intimate glimpses and interviews—"whole scenes and stretches of dialogue" to achieve Wolfe's "basic units of reporting." There seems to be involved here a process that approaches the psychoanalytical technique. But the greater, the much greater part of the news concerns events, rather than personalities and obviously you cannot put a happening on the couch.

* * *

So the practice of the New Journalism is not as easy as the preaching. Now it has become more confused because the New Journalism has sprouted a fresh branch—green and somewhat wet behind the ears, called "advocacy journalism."

These "advocates" and others among the New Journalists

who discard objectivity, assign fairness doctrines to the ash can, and apply personal opinion and personality to news coverage are not reporters. True reporting, the essence of good journalism, requires a fair presentation of both sides—more than that, all sides—of a case. An advocate is one who pleads a particular cause. He may be a devil's advocate, or he may be an angel's advocate; he is usually between the depths and the skies and rarely down to earth. Unfairness inevitably results; what begins as persuasion often turns out to be only propaganda.

Two dire results flow from most "advocacy journalism." First, there is the question of bias. Ostensibly the purpose is to correct the slant of the "Establishment," the "biased" or "banal" press, and so diminish the journalistic credibility gap. But one kind of slant is not the cure for another. What changes is only the direction in which the Tower of Pisa leans, and the credibility gap becomes not narrower but wider.

The second misuse of "advocacy journalism" is in the area of effectiveness. We return to the question of objectivity. The reporter who tries his utmost to be unbiased and to give all sides a fair shake has a chance of attracting the attention of the reader and enlightening him, no matter what his ideology. The "advocate journalist's" appeal is likely to bring a response only from the like-minded and he becomes a preacher talking to the already converted. Thus, both audience and appeal are limited.

The "advocate journalists" share other hazards of the New Journalism. They become caught up emotionally with their subjects in the course of their long association with them and neutrality becomes difficult. Real judgment must not be fogged by sentiment. Surely a conclusion based on an objective array of the facts is more soundly reached than one based on probing into a subject's "thinking" or one in which "imagination" is given full rein.

Moreover, unless he takes a considerable period for investigation, how can a New Journalist arrive at a sound opinion? Surely in covering a daily story it is impossible to get enough facts, to hear enough of both sides, to form a sound judgment. A considerable amount of the shooting then is from the hip.

Moreover, these crusading journalists should realize that they have not discovered anything new; they are reverting to the near-Stone-Age of journalism. In more primitive days news columns were clogged with opinion, making it difficult for the reader to dig out the facts. Then came objective journalism, making the sharp difference between the editorial page and the news columns. This was a distinct advance and added to the stature of journalism and its credibility without sacrifice of color or flavor.

"New" and "advocate" journalists are reverting to these darker ages. Much of their product is actual instead of factual fiction, research is scanty and sporadic, there are flights of fancy phrases; in short, these "journalists" perform as sociologists or psychoanalysts rather than as reporters.

What they overlook too is that what they call the "Old" journalism is in process of important change. Increasing emphasis is being put on interpretation—the effort to make the news clear and relevant for the reader and, whenever possible to provide an approximation of the truth. Reporting in depth is taking place in increasing degree—profiles with insights, round-ups, trend stories.

Such pieces do not appear as often as they should but a start has surely been made. Reporters and editors have definitely progressed. Publishers have still a way to go, even though they have advanced quite a distance since the days of Frank Munsey, that wholesale buyer and burier of newspapers on whose death William Allen White wrote: "Frank Munsey contributed to the journalism of his day the talents of a meat packer, the morals of a moneychanger, and the manners of an undertaker. He and his kind have about succeeded in transforming a once-noble profession into an eight per cent security. May he rest in trust."

The New Journalists should take note of these steps forward and should not believe they have all the answers. For many who use their label do not meet the basic tests of journalism; these are the alleged writers who apparently would substitute for the "who-what-when-where-how-and-why"—for these eternal and absolute basics—a large "if." This may be an exercise in freedom of the press but it certainly is not a practice consonant with press responsibility.

Only if it is responsible as well as free, will journalism fulfill its function as the Fourth Estate and remain a main bulwark of democracy. Integrity, accuracy, fairness—these are the three vital elements. The motto is supplied by Mark Twain: "Always do right. This will gratify some people and astonish the rest."

LESTER MARKEL *has been a major figure in American journalism for half a century. For forty-two years he was Sunday editor for* The New York Times. *In 1965 he became associate editor. Since his retirement from the* Times *he has remained active as a critic-commentator on the media.*

According to Gay Talese, in his book about the Times, *Markel was an extraordinary editor who ruled the Sunday* Times *with a firm belief in his own views. The firmness of his convictions has not left him in recent years. In his article Markel argues strongly that there are in the New Journalism more sins than virtues. In particular he argues that traditional journalism—the striving for objectivity in reporting—is the only road for journalism if it is to adequately serve the needs of our society.*

Markel is a graduate of City College and the Columbia School of Journalism. He is the author of several books, including What You Don't Know Can Hurt You.

9 The Necessity of Conventional Journalism: A Blend of the Old and the New

By Robert B. Semple Jr.

AS I REFLECT on the clash of views between the "old" and "new" journalism, it occurs to me that I am somewhere in the midstream. It is not that I am too old to understand the New Journalism, or too young to appreciate the virtues of the old. But I work for an institution which, like so many other members of what is loosely known as the "mass media," seems to be caught between the importunings of the New Journalism to convey a higher truth about events and the plea of the old journalists to set things forth in cold stenographic terms.

I am, in a way, surprised by the sound and fury. There is room enough in this world for objective journalism as we know it and as it survives in the *Congressional Quarterly*, the *National Journal*, the baseball results, the census reports, the stockmarket tables, and in some newspaper stories. The New Journalism seems also to be flourishing and growing, not only in *The New*

York Review of Books but in parts of *Newsweek* and *Time*, the *Nation*, *New Yorker*, the *National Review*, and lest we forget it, the *Rolling Stone*.

There is no need to fear then for the old journalism or the new. What I fear for is my kind of journalism. What I work for might be vaguely called Conventional Journalism, which satisfies neither the heretics nor the old establishment. I work for *The New York Times*, but in a sense, I work for the most of the daily newspapers in this country and for the three networks and even the radio stations. We of the midstream are under seige and we are desperately trying to adjust. One difficulty is that we don't know precisely which way to go and we are not even certain that anyone cares. We cannot write, as Norman Mailer does, "History as Novel." We cannot write as Jack Newfield does, "Journalism as Politics or Opinion." We sense, like Mailer, that we are from time to time corrupted by having to report the events that we cover, but the difficulty is that for a variety of reasons we cannot escape those events. The principal reason we cannot escape them is that if we did, there would be no mass media. We remain the backbone of the industry as it exists, and we are under pressure.

First, we are under fire from the conservatives. Recently, I appeared on what must be one of the least-watched shows on educational television with Jim Keogh, President Nixon's chief speech writer. Keogh has written a book on *Nixon and the Press*, which is essentially a compendium of all the administration's grievances against what it considers to be the "establishment" press. The moderator was James Jackson Kilpatrick of the Washington Evening Star Syndicate who, halfway through the show, became less a moderator than an ally of his guest. Both complained of a liberal bias in the so-called establishment press; both complained of too much editorializing in the news columns; both complained of reporters who are "inherently" anti-Nixon, and both complained that conventional journalism had moved too far from telling it straight to a position of advocacy.

We are also under fire from the left, or at least from the theoreticians of the New Journalism. That includes not only Nat

Hentoff who has made a good living and a good reputation in the *Village Voice* talking about the inequities and oversights of the *Times*, but from members of the *Times* like Tom Wicker and from the editors of (*more*), the journalism review. It is their view that we are patsies for official deceits, suckers for official rhetoric, painfully slow to react to obvious deceptions, purveyors of the official line, and carriers in the name of objectivity of the dread disease of establishment politics.

In short, the *Times*, and the rest of the media which it seems to represent, satisfies neither side. The right says that we are unnecessarily savage to Mr. Nixon; the left says we are too soft. In a recent issue of (*more*), Richard Harris remarked that if the presidency is a bully pulpit, then the Washington press corps is an automatic sound system.

Obviously there is much to agree with in the criticisms of those who feel somehow trapped in the middle. As the New Journalists suggest, we are often too tolerant and too uncritical of official explanations for faraway events; witness our coverage of the war in Vietnam. Most particularly witness our coverage or non-coverage of those events and decisions that were later exposed in the Pentagon Papers. It is equally true, as Mr. Keogh and others complain, that we tend to emphasize the negative while ignoring the positive. There is a telling example in Keogh's book. Every year the President of the United States gives out awards to people under the age of 21 for individual acts of bravery and heroism. Those are widely unreported awards. But one year a young girl came through the line and as we were standing there, she walked up to the President and said, "Mr. President, I really can't believe in you until you end the war in Vietnam." And suddenly that award ceremony made page 1—four columns, in fact, at the bottom of the page, under my by-line. And Keogh asked in his book whether I would have been equally excited if the girl had walked up to the President and said, "Mr. President, I cannot support you until you unleash maximum American firepower to end this war in Vietnam." The sheer novelty of that situation would have at least interested me and, I hope, sparked some interest among my editors, but basically Jim Keogh has a point.

If the lonely voice of someone in the middle may be permitted some response to its critics on both sides, I would suggest several things. One of them is that establishment attitudes and ideology play less of a role and govern less of what we do than people normally suspect. Whatever the reporter's personal feelings about Richard Nixon are, sooner or later some code of professionalism tends to take over when that reporter sits down at the typewriter. Further, many of the things we do emerge not from conviction or political attitudes but from other human traits—stupidity, laziness, inadequacy.

Keogh spends a great deal of time in his book criticizing *The New York Times* for its failure to report the Nixon administration's effort to channel more and more money into black colleges and then, a month later, playing on page 1 a story quoting black educators who were critical of the Nixon administration for not supporting their colleges. That happened only because of the following sequence of events. The announcement of the original grants was made at six o'clock at the White House. I had two other stories to do. I recommended that we either use the AP or UPI to cover the story. The editor did not get the message and the story never ran. Keogh elevates that into an illustration of the *Times'* emotional and political bias against the Nixon administration, when in fact it was the fault, essentially, of a reporter who felt he had other priorities.

I would like to suggest one other reason for our troubles which is probably far more fundamental. Ideology may lead us into trouble with some groups whom we pain and irritate over a period of time. Stupidity may enrage our critics on a given day. Our professionalism and alleged objectivity may cause us to seem unnecessarily bland and unexciting when compared to Tom Wolfe or Jack Newfield. But our chief burden is that we have been trying to tell the news and this causes of lot of trouble because nobody has ever defined what informing the reader is.

James Reston once said that the journalist is trapped somewhere between a trade, like bricklaying or plumbing, and a profession, such as law or medicine. But unlike either the trades or the higher professions, journalists do not have particularly well-written codes and standards of behavior. And it is, in practical terms, impossible to do so. Therefore, with one foot in the past, the so-called objective tradition, and one foot tentatively creeping toward the future of the New Journalism, we have simply tried our best to improvise. There have been two obvious results of that improvisation process. One has been the rise of so-called interpretative journalism in places like the *Times*. Possibly the only major media which still shun it are the two wire services which treat interpretation as gingerly as they would treat advocacy and opinion.

Let me mention one minor example to demonstrate how far I think we have come, not just on our editorial pages, but in the news columns themselves. Some time ago, after considerable public pressure, Mr. Nixon finally released a message on school busing. He appeared on nationwide television and the next day dispatched to Congress a document of considerably greater length. I wrote that story and did essentially three things. First, I tried to set forth the facts of what Nixon did. Second, I tried to give some history in the story about where his ideas had come from, and third I tried to suggest his political motives and ultimate ambitions. The day after the message came out I did a long piece on the history and the day after that I did a news analysis on the political motives. But what interests me is that on the first day I felt free enough to try to do all three things in what used to be a conventional news story. The difficulty again is that this has not satisfied either set of critics. The political left and some elements of the New Journalism would deplore the amount of space that we concede to the administration's program to begin with and would wish more immediate judgment and advocacy one way or the other, and the administration people would resent what little interpretation was tried.

The television industry is hardly exempt from these complaints. Because it is so visible (and for most of us even inescapable) television news has been the focus of even greater criticism than we have. This criticism arises from essentially the same phenomenon—namely the effort of those in the middle to combine, in one news report, the perceived facts of a situation and some interpretation of the meaning and motives behind those facts. Critics of the President, however, tend to resent the amount of time which television gives him. His admirers, meanwhile, are amazed when the television industry has the effrontery to use some of that time to comment on what he has said.

A second manifestation of our efforts to move forward without damaging our roots is an increasingly heavy emphasis on investigative reporting. There are those who call it the New Muckraking. But it is only a somewhat higher and more energetic form of a kind of investigative reporting that has long been honored in the business. To demonstrate the fact that greater emphasis is now being given investigative work, one need only look at the composition of the Washington Bureau of *The New York Times*. Seymour Hersh recently became the fourth full-time investigative man. Bob Smith is doing Justice and ITT and was before the scandal broke. Walter Rugaber does this work on a general assignment basis. And, of course, Neil Sheehan could not have unearthed the Pentagon Papers unless the *Times* had been committed to that kind of journalism. The interesting thing about this is that, in the past, the *Times* tended to approach investigative reporting on an essentially catch as catch can basis—when those who were responsible for the daily flow of news had a little extra time or when they inadvertently and reluctantly stumbled over a set of classified documents. But now it is a full-time proposition.

We have not worked out a great many of our problems. We are torn between our historic demands for quantity, and I am referring not just to the *Times* but to all newspapers and even television in this country, and particularly the wire services, and increasing pressures to produce longer pieces of quality. We have come late to the New Muckraking and there is far more to be done. One of the greatest confessions of press failure was the notoriety achieved by Ralph Nader with the publication of *Unsafe At Any Speed*. If I had to pick a so-called New Journalist who I thought had made the greatest impact on those of us somewhere in the middle, it would be Nader, because he singlehandedly started doing the job which the press ought to have been doing for most of its history. He has done much to illuminate the culture of the bureaucracy in Washington, D.C., its successes and its short-comings, and the press has not. He put the consumer issue on the map, and the press did not. But even though we came late to it, we are still moving at an increasingly rapid pace towards a higher form of investigative reporting, which will be useful and will continue to attract the attention and the talent of the people coming into the business. The kind of news that not only tells the reader what happened but gives him some guidance and perspective, without at the same time being tendentious or advocating a particular position, remains as necessary today as it always has.

Beyond that I am interested in reporting that breaks new ground. I admire and value the the deployment of resources in the *Times* and in other journals that produced not only the Pentagon Papers but the first revelation of the relationship between ITT and the administration. From these two episodes emerged one of the first thoughtful examinations in some time of the relationship between the government and the press.

In sum, I think there is room for all three of us—for the pure objectivists (though their numbers are dwindling); for advocacy journalism, which produces a kind of writing which we are still not equipped to handle, and finally, for my kind of journalism, which is the journalism of the mass media. I am not saying that we are really good at it yet, but I think we are working at it.

ROBERT SEMPLE JR. is the deputy national news editor and former White House correspondent for The New York Times. In his article, Semple argues for something he has labelled Conventional Journalism—the kind of journalism he believes The New York Times is producing today.

Conventional Journalism, according to Semple, lies somewhere between old, objective journalism and new, advocacy journalism. Semple's journalism, journalism of the mass media he calls it, does not become the opinion of the reporter but neither does it wear the blinders of objective journalism. The conventional journalist ought to be alert enough to the real world to sense official mendacity, to ferret it out and to report it if it exists. But he does not simply assume its existence and then report his assumption.

Semple began working for The New York Times in 1963. Before that he worked for the Wall Street Journal and the National Observer. He received a BA from Yale University and an MA from the University of California at Berkeley.

10 The Underground Press: Notes on the Past and the Future

By Brian Boyer

TWO DAILY NEWSPAPERMEN and their uncertain friend, an underground journalist, recently went hunting for bear in a wilderness area. After spending several days in the thickets and not finding game, the fellow from the underground sheet volunteered to scout new territory. The other two more conventional men agreed to let him go but decided to remain where they were and wait for the bear to come to them. Several hours after the independent journalist had wandered off, the two remaining hunters spied a menacing form some distance away at the edge of the wood. Assuming it was a bear they both fired and hit their mark. When they rushed up for their quarry, they discovered they had shot the underground journalist. The victim was, however, still drawing breath. The two newspapermen went to work on the victim the way the book said—packed him in the car and rushed him to the nearest hospital. After many hours of anxious waiting, the two hunters stood up when the attending physician walked in glumly from the operating room. "I am afraid," the doctor said, "your friend has gone to his reward." "That's terrible," the newspapermen cried. "We didn't mean to shoot him and we got him to the hospital as fast as we could. He *was* unconventional, but we liked him. Tell us, doctor, is there anything we could have done to save him before we took him out of the woods?" "Well, there is one little thing," the doctor said, "it would have helped if you hadn't gutted him first."

I have spent most of five years in some of the country's larger metropolitan morning newspapers, and at least an equal amount of time with what most journalists would call the underground press. Correctly, this other press is called the Alternative Press. Its practitioners are then alternative journalists, and what they write about could even be called alternative news. The phrases set a fascinating duality—the idea there are two news worlds. One of them is the embodiment of the conventional wisdom and it is by definition an economically rewarded major medium. The other one may or may not have any wisdom at all. It certainly does not have the status or the money enjoyed by its richer cousin. In addition, what the big fellow holds sacred, the poor relation scorns. The first is designed to appeal to the average and homogenized man with the average IQ of an eleven-year-old. The second may very well be read by eleven-year-olds, but it is designed to appeal to more literate, albeit unconventional adults—people at least with adult brains. The rich one finally opposed the war in Vietnam for the most part. The poor one vehemently hated it from the start. The big one masks its prejudices and the small one flaunts them. Each has its own flaws; neither one is very good.

The underground press at least has the honesty to print what it believes is the truth while the conventional newspaper practices hypocrisy with the conviction of an American President who pleads that people who fight back are aggressors.

The established press worships at the conventional headwaters of wisdom, the official source. Consider this example. An informant of a newspaper reporter with whom I am acquainted, recently went out and murdered a real estate woman for whom the informant worked. The woman had plans to kill him for confiding in the reporter. The background is a Federal Housing Administration scandal. It is a major national story ignored by most of the press for two years because of its complexity and perhaps because of the complex relationships between newspapers, banks and the mortgage companies. In any case, the man who used the chrome-plated .38 to send the bullet between the lady's eyes, had sat with the reporter through many a long night in a deserted city room. He had specific and important information about individuals who broke laws in the FHA scandal. He also explained to the reporter his conflicting feelings about the woman he subsequently murdered. The man's information was so valuable that the reporter made his informant available to a CBS television news producer who flew across the country to film the man for his own FHA coverage.

The night before the man was to appear before the cameras, the informant called the producer and told him he had just murdered a woman in a real estate office. The producer called the reporter and then confirmed that the woman he suspected could be the victim—indeed was. From the producer he got a detailed account of the man's conversations—conversations that clearly explained the motives of the crime and the circumstances that led up to it. The reporter at the murderer's home spoke with the man's wife who corroborated with even more detail the producer's story. Both the producer and the wife were told by the murderer that he had killed the real estate lady. Then the police reporter talked to the policeman who had interviewed witnesses to the crime and got their story. The murderer had been taken into police custody almost immediately.

The reporter had everything he needed for a sensational murder story with much more significant overtones. But a senior editor at the newspaper who had great faith in the conventional news processes, refused to allow the true reports of the murderer's confessions into the newspaper on the ground that those reports were not official. They had not come from the police. This decision was made despite the assurance of the newspaper's libel lawyer that no libel whatsoever was involved in telling the story. In addition, the same editor made a decision for the sake of the conventional wisdom to delete all of the reporter's detailed knowledge about the murderer and his business and emotional relationships to the victim.

This is tantamount to not printing the Pentagon Papers because they are apparently true. What was printed was not a detailed and fascinating account of a murder over a quarrel about FHA, but a police story which simply said—Mary Smith was slain and John Doe is being held. All the news, I suppose, that's fit to print.

Why did the editor play the story as he did? Because, the editor said later, the official story is the safe one and the one to go with even when firsthand knowledge of the events would cause one to disagree. Furthermore, he said, he recognized that the official version of things is frequently misleading or false but he said sometimes the truth does come out in official stories and then the news story develops. But it does not develop, he implied, by a newspaperman's initiative. Nor does the truth get told apparently if the official source doesn't want it to be told. This decision he thought was a responsible one. It may not have created a very good story but it had one virtue that overshadowed everything. A story done his way, he said, couldn't be wrong. It could be a tissue of lies, errors and misstatements and self-justification by the officials but because it came from the official mouthpiece, it was right. You would be surprised at the number of reporters and editors who still share that same attitude—right or wrong.

There you have why I came into journalism, what keeps me in it—the fight over right and wrong, fact and fancy, objective correlative vs. hogwash. It is astonishing really, that man's argument. It is the same argument presented to me by another editor on December 4, 1969 when police killed a Black Panther named Fred Hampton in his sleep. On that day officials told reporters that Hampton died in the midst of a violent gun battle with policemen who were serving a warrant after a vicious attack by the Black Panthers on the peaceful police. I learned only hours after the killing by going to the scene and compulsively going over the evidence found there that police had fired hundreds of shots into the apartment where Hampton and another man were killed, but the vicious criminals inside had apparently fired none at all. For the sake of the record, let me say that evidence was found later of one shot fired from inside the apartment. Of a gunbattle, there was none.

Shortly after I quit the *Chicago Sun-Times* because of its mistaken decision to banner the official story and bury the factual one, the *Chicago Tribune* printed official photographs of the murder scene. Those official photographs which were supposed to prove that the Panthers had fired at the police showed in fact only nails pounded into a door. Then the *Sun-Times* picked up the phony *Tribune* photographs and two newspapers, which should have known better, proudly fed the public official lies with their breakfast cereal. The photograph-con did embarrass the newspapers enough that they began doing what the *Chicago Journalism Review* had already done—investigating the facts of the story and looking for the truth in places other than the official documents. Underground journalists make mistakes of many kinds but those caused by too much trust in official sources are few.

Why mistrust official sources? Because the simple misrepresentations of reality which government sources used to hand out now have become bolder and colder lies. The government's position now, unless the truth reverberates to its own advantage, is to lie outright even when the lie has no immediate apparent benefit. Optimistic assessments of South Vietnam's fighting capacities became such an old, obvious lie, one wonders why it was served up so frequently. Apparently our newspapers have a hankering for junk food. Look at some of the other lies brought to us by official sources. How about the story about the inexorable decline of our central cities, instead of decline brought about by individuals? Or the one about the middle man's profit in high meat prices, when there is no middle man? Or the public utility of Amtrak or the SST or the practical utility of moon exploration?

Lies about these topics and many others are given out even before questions are asked to prevent anyone from getting close to the facts in the first place. But come closer to home and look at

some lies. Lies about how much it costs to run a city, for example, when tax-free dollars go out to bond holders, who are being paid for lending money at prohibitive prices when the government could finance capital improvements with direct grants. Lies about how sports stadiums support themselves when they actually take direct tax money and offer huge tax-free loopholes in the form of fast appreciation. Lies by police about the basic honesty of policemen when every urban dweller knows that cops openly solicit bribes for heroin, whores, gambling, traffic tickets and who knows what else. There is no end to them. I don't know if there always have been lies, but I believe that they will go on forever until we sustain an atomic attack and our official sources proclaim another victory, much in the way our generals continued to proclaim victory in Vietnam against the stupid and incompetent North Vietnamese. The overground press prints the lies; the underground press doesn't, not those lies at any rate. This is not to vilify the overground print media but to suggest that its members adopt logic instead of slogans, and keep a critical eye on facts.

The overground is adopting some of the salutary features of the alternative media, while, of all things, underground publications are going legitimate. To give you an example of how the overground press is turning under, look to the working press. In my city room is a Black Panther, a member of the radical rainbow people's party, a populist who really knows his marks in economics, an avowed socialist, a radical conservative, a Buckley backer and half a dozen other reporters who were trained in the underground press. These are good reporters and good writers who are not polemicists. When they have a position to advocate they pick their stories carefully to illustrate it, true stories that do not come from the official sources. Wherever there are young journalists, good writers—male and female, under and sometimes over 30 years old, you will find the folks who brought you the *Chicago Seed*, the *Detroit Fifth Estate* and *Los Angeles Free Press*. When this isn't literally true, although a goodly number of counter-culturalists have joined in an economic relationship with the established press, nearly all of the young journalists are from the college newspapers that are more underground now than underground sheets were five years ago.

At the same time the underground sheets are moving to the right. Dozens of the underground newspapers that flourished only months ago have folded their pages and gone to the big recycling plant in the sky. They did it for two reasons. Because political crazies took over and drove the writing talent out and because, in the nature of attrition the more successful ones drove the weaker ones out, just like bad news drives out good news. Take the *Rolling Stone*, which *Playboy* would dearly love to pay $4 million for and mint money from. It has the circulation now of fifty independent underground newspapers and has absorbed much of the former underground audience in fifty cities. It succeeded because it is much better than those it drove out. If it continues to grow and develop news stories, the *Rolling Stone* could become America's first true national newspaper. The *National Observer* is not.

Also successful are the *Phoenix* in Boston, *Daily Planet* in Chicago, and the sturdy *Free Press* in Los Angeles to name a few. The *Daily Planet* was created by my former partner in the *Chicago Free Press*, a short-lived but lively weekly magazine. Unlike the *Free Press*, the *Daily Planet* has kept its costs low and its advertising revenues high. It is now making money with a biweekly paying public of about 30,000. The *Phoenix* circulates 70,000, and makes money. The *Los Angeles Free Press* makes enough money to be able to afford labor disputes.

Now there are two other kinds of alternative journals that fascinate me as much as the underground newspapers. They are the exploitational press and the classified shopper. The exploitation press is a broad spectrum of tabloid newspapers, with circulation ranging from the millions down to a few thousand. They are as chaste as the *National Inquirer* is now, and as raw as *Screw*. There is even a humor sheet in the zoo, a paper whose jokes appeal to sexual deviates. What is fascinating about publications like the *Inquirer* and the *Enquirer*, different publications which by no accident sound almost exactly alike, is when they cleaned up to get into grocery store magazine racks, they also found a

HAIGHT–ASHBURY
FREE PRESS

25¢
35¢
OUTSIDE
BAY AREA

VOL. 2 NO. 2 (UPS)   SAN FRANCISCO GRAPHIC ARTS SOCIETY   1778 HAIGHT STREET

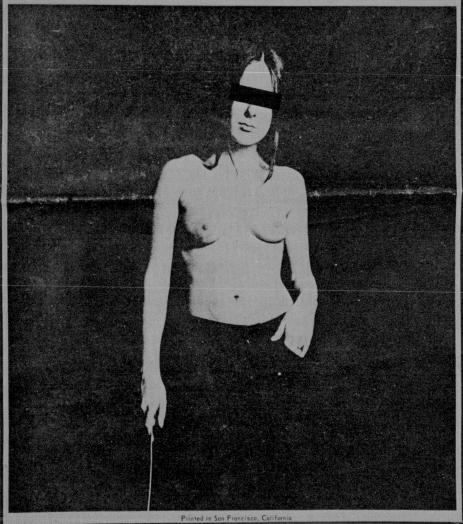

Printed in San Francisco, California

mass audience. The mass audience that reads these newspapers probably would not rank among our most literate publics. But it is not entirely composed of dullards as some think. Most of its readers are working people with a strong mistrust of official news of any kind because officials usually lie to them with monotonous regularity. The exploitational press also draws circulation from the conventional newspapers. Its readers, many of whom are unwilling to read a newspaper every day, are the old Hearst crowd, which nobody seems to care about any more. They like simple things—scandal in high places, confirmation of their beliefs that the government is largely composed of thieves, crime, domestic tragedy and sex. It is a pretty good combination actually.

The classified shopper has become a real part of my life. It is a tabloid which usually prints nothing but classified advertisements. You know like "Good stove, avocado, gas, like new, $50. Call after 6 p.m." Advertisers do not pay for their space in advance. Instead they pay a small percentage or $2 minimum, whichever is higher, after a piece is sold. The selling price of the publication is usually twenty-five cents, and in cities such as Detroit, Cleveland, Columbus, and parts of Chicago and in New York City, they are now selling by the thousands. They have two things going for them—high reader interest and a service to both buyers and sellers. Economically they also make sense because the reader throws down his quarter gladly for the newspaper's content and the advertiser stands in line to get his material in figuring it is free even when it is not.

The future of the classified shopper should be good. The reason for the bright future is that they have started printing editorial material—news if you will. And its basic economic success has given it the freedom to be as iconoclastic and independent as its publisher-editor is. Because the advertisers in these shoppers come by the thousands rather than by the dozens, the harm caused by anyone angered enough by a story to pull his advertising out is nil. So the publication would be subject to no external economic pressures. It is possible for a classified shopper to establish itself as a major metropolitan daily newspaper someplace down the road. I believe that is exactly what's going to happen.

Despite the bad examples, many newspapers are starting to get a bone-ache when an official talks about the truth. Most newsmen believe participants and first-person observers better than they do second-hand sources whose knowledge consists of reports—sometimes reports of reports. The overground press is not changing rapidly, but it is altering, melting like a frozen ice on a hot July day as younger reporters and a different kind of reader bring on the heat. I doubt that the underground and overground will mate and the product slither off toward some kingdom of Id and Oz, and I would not actually want it to. But there is no reason why a hybrid with much vigor and good taste could not appear. The hybrid will be a glad-hearted, curious and independent soul who, of course, will lie once in a while—not for profit, but just because it felt like it. Most of all it will be impatient of lies and also willing to run the facts over the curiosities. One story may take an entire issue once in a while, as *The New York Times* should have done with the Pentagon Papers. Readers will like it and reporters will like it too. It will have a spirit like ripple wine. Ripple, for those who are too sophisticated to know, is an alcoholic soda pop with a red color, a clean taste and a 99-cent price tag—bright, fresh and cheap. That is the way a newspaper ought to be.

It reminds me of the old *Literary Times*, more than a decade ago. The *Literary Times* was a child of the late Ben Hecht who was a great newspaperman from Chicago. A quarter of a century after its publishing reserves were drunk up in an excess of joy, a wild man named Jay Robert Nash, a spitting image of James Cagney, persuaded Hecht to give him the title rights. In the 1960's Nash, who would strike the man who called him a beat or hippy, preferring to be an anchorite to the lost generation, began the modern underground press from a $10 office in Chicago on North Clark Street. Of course it wasn't Nash alone, but there were not that many people—no, there were virtually none. The sheet had no reverence. It mocked the great, investigated the holy, was critical of the dead and made news. At best it had a monthly circulation of 10,000 which Nash promoted as 30,000. It was a damned important publication.

The *New York Review of Books* and other intellectual sheets were all influenced by it. Nash says that he created the underground, but he is an egotist—influenced it is good enough. When the time came that it threatened to make money, he killed it out of pity. He thought his newspaper was selling him out. We had tight standards in those days. It was too early to be successful at the wholehearted approach to the news so the *Literary Times* died. The fact is that every publication I have been associated with on an intimate level in the underground has died. The exception is the *Chicago Journalism Review,* but that one was intended to be nonprofit. Knowledge gained at the graveside is true knowledge, however. The undergrounds are the vehicles of the future—bitter, defeatest, accurate. All this comes to us like a note from the underground. Help!—it reads, we are all prisoners. Only the word will make us free.

When BRIAN BOYER writes of the underground press—or alternative journalism as he feels it should be called—he knows whereof he writes. Boyer has had more than five years experience with the undergrounds—most of it with publications which ultimately failed financially. As he has written elsewhere, "I have built a vision of the kingdom and the power to come on broken crockery shards."

In his present article Boyer suggests that the establishment media have already been affected by the undergrounds—if only because a number of underground journalists now work in establishment newsrooms. And in fact the undergrounds themselves, at least the more successful of them, are becoming more establishment-like. He suggests, hopefully, that there may someday be a kind of hybrid newspaper combining the best of both press worlds.

Boyer has worked for the Literary Times, the Chicago Free Press, Chicago Journalism Review, Chicago Sun-Times, and the Detroit Free Press. He is the author of Cities Destroyed for Cash and a series of detective books under the general title, The Head Hunters.

11 | Selections from the Underground Press

IT IS NOT POSSIBLE to suggest the scope and variety of the underground press through a few pictures and articles taken from the undergrounds. The variety was and is too great. There are papers for and about lesbians, for and about homosexuals, promoting women's rights, promoting the black movement. There are crusading undergrounds; there are undergrounds which are simply anti-establishment; there are undergrounds promoting free sex and/or the drug cult. Some of the undergrounds seem to combine a bit of all these interests; others confine themselves quite narrowly to one interest.

What can be sensed through a few examples are some of the differences between the undergrounds and the mass media. Consider three areas: page design, writing style and subject matter treatment. The page design, like most other elements, is inconsistent—though largely non-conventional. In quality, page design runs from that which appears to have been put together by a graphics artist to that in which the prime concern seems to have been merely putting words into the paper. One finds full-page

Editor's Note: The following selections contain language which most would call coarse, at best. If the reader objects to such language, he is advised to skip this section. The selections are included because they illustrate the manner in which the undergrounds approach journalism.

harry

25¢

"Those who carry a peace sign in one hand and a bomb or a brick in the other are the super-hypocrites of our time."

—Richard Nixon

Albuquerque, Oct. 31, 1970

pictures, hand written script, type set into circles or triangles—
and occasionally something which even looks like a newspaper.

The writing style is usually very personal and therefore
highly idiosyncratic. There is very little traditional, inverted
pyramid, begin-with-the-most-important-element news style. Instead one finds impressionistic pieces, personal essays, chron-
ological narratives—even poetry and short stories. Any style may
be appropriate. The writer generally uses the style which allows
him to express the message as he wishes to express it.

Finally subject matter. We have already suggested the
variety. The subject matter is usually that which the establishment press won't handle—or will handle in only the most cautious manner. Sex is one rather obvious example. Of course, establishment papers deal with sex—frequently. But their handling is
most often either extremely circumspect or designed to titillate.
The underground treatment may titillate, but it is forthright.
Drugs are another example. In the establishment press, when
drugs are dealt with it is usually in a factual and/or negative
sense ("Narcotics Ring Broken" or "Youth Dies of Overdose").
Rarely, if ever are drugs handled as an accepted item. In the undergrounds, they are often treated in a friendly fashion.

GAY PRIDE WEEK*

Staying with friends in Madison, N.J. Stoned, really stoned,
and it's late at night, and I'm listening to some New York FM station and these people from Gay Liberation Front are rapping
about Gay Pride week and it does my heart good, 'cause I'm a
freaking Fag revolutionary and I'm lonely and horney and tomorrow morning I'm going to New York to see my Gay brothers and
sisters and help fight this oppression.

Baltimore Gay Liberation Front is here. Right on. Beautiful
blonde in a redwhiteandblue almost shirt tells me to eat. None of
this New Mobe fruit and breadcrust shit. Beef stroganoff, rice
curry, tossed salad with sour cream—Outasight. . . . Workshop

*From *Harry*, July 17, 1970, p. 4.

on sexism and Women's Lib. . . . Freaks carrying signs "I am a Homosexual" on the street, approaching straights and inviting them to carry it for a block and see what it feels like. . . . Music and dancing—brothers and sisters getting it together. Walk with a beautiful brother arm in arm to Alternate U for discussion by Gay Socialist Red Butterfly. . . . Some straight playing tapes of goldenoldies shit. Liberate the music. Three Dog Night is speeding and my gay brothers are dancing, moving, smoking, balling, talking.

It's Sunday and 6th Ave. is clear for the march to Central Park for the Gay-in. Old and young and queens and studs and militant gays and drag queens and all Gay brothers and sisters are united and walking 10,000 strong. Don't get in our way motherfuckers. We'll trample you. Come out! Come Out! Out of the closets and into the streets! G.L.F. is marching hard and sisters and brothers are smoking and rapping and dancing in the street and central park is parting for us and I'm at the top of the hill and I stop and turn around and I see my Gay people 10,000 strong and proud and I cry and feel good. Making it in the park and digging on the together vibes and the clear blue sky. Everybody felt it then. A quiet fell over our heads. There will be no more happy days for us until every day can be a happy day for us. All of us. Without the necessary support of numbers. Our oppressed brothers and sisters—black, red, brown, gray—we are all together now. And we'll fight to the last drop of blood for our freedom. All power to the people. All power to the Gay people. Unite with us Gay brothers and sisters and help us fuck Amerika.

CONFESSIONS OF A SEXPLOITED LADY
By Little Bare*

"The one titled feature was called 'Free Ride' and it featured a young man getting just that—in bed with a willing girl."—San Francisco Examiner

I got into the "willing girl" business several months ago because I needed some bread in a bad way. I worked exclusively for

*From *Berkeley Tribe,* Aug. 23-29, 1969, p. 9.

FEDS AMBUSH SEALE *See Page 3*

BERKELEY TRIBE

PUBLISHED BY THE STAFF OF THE FORMER BARB

PUBLISHED WEEKLY BY RED MOUNTAIN TRIBE   P.O. BOX 9043, BERKELEY, CA. 94709   WALLER PRESS 182   VOL. 1 NO. 7 ISSUE 7 AUG. 22-28, 1969   15¢ BAY AREA   25¢ ELSEWHERE

WILD HOGS RAID S.F. SKIN FLICKS!

BANG! EXIT OINK! SOCK!

CHEEZIT! THE PIGS!

SEE STORY ON PAGE 9

LUNDGREN—GRIMSHAW

one theater for three weeks averaging a movie every four or five days and got average pay—about $50 for seven hours work.

I quit working for this outfit when the bad shit that was coming down became too much to take—a friend of the theater owner, whose apartment we were using to film a lez flick—attacked one of the other chicks as she was leaving the pad. He ripped all her clothes off and started to beat on her.

The owner of the theater, who the assholes at KFRC periodically interview as a "prominent man about town," stood there laughing and scratching his balls.

Later, while driving back to the theater, he said "that guy's really getting funny; he pulled the same thing in the theater the other day."

The funny thing is that the first time I worked for the guy, a sister actress warned me that he was the shittiest person in the business and told me no one worked for him until they became so overexposed that no one else would hire them.

During the next couple of weeks, I worked for five other filmmakers who could be described like this:

1) A groovy lady who made no demands and paid better ($60—3 hours) than anyone else. She used to be a model and knows where the chicks who have to do this are at. The last I heard, Reagan and his pigs had paranoided her out of the business.

2) A gay who doesn't want any chick to forget that he's the biggest nelly queen bitch that ever lived. He demands the girls think up plots and dialogue for three movies before they're even hired. He pays average money.

3) An egocentrical aging teeny-bopper who takes his business just a little too seriously and who averages two lays a week from among his models—an average he works hard at maintaining. He pays average. One of my films was confiscated when the pigs busted his customers last week; it showed me swimming in a pool and then going up to my apartment and playing with myself. Like all other scenes of this type, it is so directed that you're playing with yourself in a manner that no chick from Eve forward could possibly enjoy. I often wonder why these cats are afraid to

110

film a woman really playing with herself? His place is one block off the San Francisco financial district, and was raided at 5:45 p.m. I also wonder why the pigs didn't come stomping in during lunch hour and bust some bankers and such.

4) A straight cat who is just in business to make money. He drives his models harder than anyone else, but it's in the interest of turning on the patrons (clowns, as they're commonly called in the business) rather than himself. His pay is very little, five or six bills an hour.

5) Another straight cat who's trying to make it on his own after working as a photographer for some of the worst people in town. He pays about $15 for a 90-minute session but is constantly hassled by his wife, who's afraid their rich Orinda neighbors will find out what he does for a living.

6) A kindly, dirty-old-man type who can't get over the fact that Tempest Storm got her start as a stripper in his Oakland Burly Q parlor. He pays well and takes color Polaroids of you for his album. If you and the cat you're working with put on a good show (like, go down on each other) you get more money, but he's cool enough not to ask you to do it.

Basically, those are the types of bosses in the business. Personally, I think the movies are shitty. They all depict women as being very low, vile creatures and something to be totally despised, with absolutely no worth as people.

The girls all feel we're not getting paid enough for all the shit we have to do.

Shit like the one guy who once got a bunch of chicks working on a flick in his theater lobby and then invited the customers out to watch.

"How do you like that," he'd say, grabbing a tit, or, "What do you think of that ass, fella."

According to a chick who was there, it was just like an ol'time slave auction.

Another bastard, who I don't think is working anymore, used to get girls to pose for one movie and tell them he wanted to shoot the second half after they'd shaved their cunt. No shave, no bread.

111

There's been loose talk of organizing a union or something, but none of us want to get busted, so we'd rather keep our names out of the papers and things.

You can't really afford to get busted, because if you do you're out there all alone, baby. It's not like topless where there is usually a company lawyer.

There's a big shot in LA that owns about 20 theaters, five or six in Frisco, he won't even back his managers if they're busted in a raid.

It's too fucking much how all of these guys claim that they're the only ones trying to make real sincere films about love.

Horseshit.

None of them that I've ever worked for (including two generally thought to be the best in the area) try to attain any realism in love.

Every move, every gesture is a calculated effort to titillate or arouse the audience.

They'll tell you to do something, like kiss your own tit, imagine, and justify it by saying "that will turn on the old farts."

They tend to think of all the audience as old impotent men or young impotent men, guys who aren't ever going to make it with the real thing. From the customers I've seen, I would guess most of them make it with someone, every now and then anyway.

One of the funniest things in the business is the use of props and gimmicks. Of course, making the girls put vasoline or spit on their cunts to look wet is common.

Other popular props are feather dusters and dildoes. Theoretically, you will be busted if you show a girl with something besides her finger in her cunt. Hence the dildoes seldom get used for real.

Despite this you still see girls fondling them a lot—in their hands and rubbing them on their thighs. Sure, Cecil B. DeMille, the whole fucking world buys $14 dildoes to rub the tips with their thumb.

Other gimmicks I have seen used are playing with yourself with toy dolls and having a feline-type cat lick a girl's bush. At

112

least that was real, the cat was damn well grooving on the cream they'd put there.

Despite all the shit, I'm still politically and morally opposed to the busts. Personally these movies bore the hell out of me, and I don't think that's the effect that real obscenity has on a person.

People have as much right to pay $4 and watch me play with four equally bored chicks and one slightly amused cat on the screen as Mayor Alioto or Ed Nevin (head of the SF vice squad) have to walk down Broadway and watch the boobs bounce.

HARRY REPORTER DROPS ACID, HEARS BILLY GRAHAM, SEE APOCALYPSE, DIGS IT

By Thomas V. D'Antoni*

Scene: July 4. The Lincoln Memorial—its alabastard columns and its simple dignity—symbolic. It's like the Parthenon, the Coleseum and the Reichstag—symbolic of an empire. Undimmed by human tears but gaddamned sooty from the pollution.

Fan back: The army chorus, senators, congressmen, Kate Smith, Bob Hope, The Army band, 4,000 hard hats, Nixon freaks, flag freaks, God's own prophet—the gospel of Amerika incarnate—Billy Graham, a huge Amerikan Flag, and your mother and father on the steps in front of the memorial. They are singing the Star Spangled Banner, which as you know is the former national anthem. Some guys somewhere in back of the memorial are firing a fifty-six gun salute.

Pan back further: Two thousand freaks on the banks of and inside the reflecting pool doing a number of interesting things including: (a) giving the scene in front of them (1) the fist, and (2) the finger; and (b) just sitting there saying "far out, far fucking out!"

*From *Harry*, July 17, 1970, p. 4

harry

25¢

Photo by LSD-25 under the influence of Tom D'Antoni

HARRY Reporter Drops Acid, Hears Billy Graham, Sees Apocalypse, Digs It.

by THOMAS V. D'ANTONI

Scene: July 4. The Lincoln Memorial, its alabastard columns and its simple dignity so symbolic. It's like the Parthenon, the Coliseum and the Reichstag. —symbolic of an empire. Enlivened by human feet but goddamned spitty from the pollution.

Pan back. The scene: chorus, anthem, compression. Karlo Smith, Bob Hope, The Army Itself is very hard here, human freaks, flag freaks, God's own prophet — the gospel of Amerika incarnate— Billy Graham, a huge Amerikan Flag, and your mother and father on the steps in front of the memorial. They are singing the Star Spangled Banner, which as you know is the former national anthem. Some guys somewhere in back of the memorial are fixing a fifty-six gun salute.

Pan back further. Two thousand freaks on the banks of and inside the reflecting pool doing a number of interesting things including: (a) giving the scene in front of them (1) the fist, and (2) the finger, and (b) just sitting there saying "far out, far fucking out!"

It seems we had the smoke-in after all.

Right! Being ripped us off, and the "movement" heavier couldn't get together, so we did what we've always done, from Woodstock to the last Balto-Cong demonstration in May — we just did it ourselves——TOGETHER.

There was no admission, there was no fences, no speeches, no collections, no march routes, and NO fucking marshals.

People started arriving as early as Thursday and the D.C. free community put them up until The Big Day. Some

crashed on the grounds of the Washington Monument on Friday night. Unfortunately they were forced to play a rather unfriendly game of hide and go pig with the local constabulary. I heard they didn't get off it too much though. Mother of fact, some of the people I talked too kind of dug it. Of course, they were stoned who I looked on them.

I arrived at dawn — shirted. There were about three hundred freaks there then including a large contingent of Yippies who were painting people's faces with orange and blue war paint. I got some of the blue, but none of the orange.

Everyone was sitting on the lawn in front of the Washington Monument smoking their funny looking cigarettes and puffing on pipes. I joined them. Far!

Was the dope good? Let me put it this way—I took fifteen pictures before I realized I had no film in my camera. Yeah, it was good dope.

By nine o'clock the crowd numbered around a thousand — all stoned. The Billy Graham Honor America Before it Honors You Buddy Day Ceremonies were getting ready at the Lincoln Memorial so I walked over to the area of the press trailer so I could get press credentials. I was prevented from doing so by a cop.

"I can't even get into the press trailer to see whether I can get credentials?" I said.

"That's right."

"Oh."

I was really stoned.

After an uneventful stroll around the reflecting pool and Lincoln Memorial—

well, I sat ea off an Amerikan flag from a vendor and tie it upside down around my ass and walked back to the Washington Monument grounds and found that the number of freaks had almost doubled. Upon entering the Yippie tent (a large truck something) and a lab of that dynamite white acid on me——FREE. Yippies are like that.

I too then on things became a little orange. Let's see—I remember ripping off a vendor for a box of Crackerjax, I remember that.

Well, I trucked on over to the Lincoln Memorial again and found that there were lots of freaks in the reflecting pool. Just then Deliverdoke Billy and Friends cranked up their Gods and began their show.

There was one disturbance at the Lincoln Memorial end of the pool when the cops and horses to keep the freaks from storming the ceremonies. Couple of people got kicked in the head by the horses. I got off.

I'm afraid you're going to have to ask your friends about the details of what happened after that because—well, I know what I saw but it's hard to tell how accurate any of this is.

For instance, I don't think the Lincoln Memorial Rally turned into the Reichstag. I mean there really weren't any Nazi flags, were there?

As far as I can figure out, these was some head busting and gassing. This may have been caused by things like the Yippies liberating a giant supermarket opening floodlight, tossing it in the pool and using it as a raft.

By the way there was a huge thunderstorm—high winds, lightning, and lots of rain. We caused that. There was so much fucking freak energy that it directed itself upwards and the fury of the heavens broke loose on Bob Hope's festivities. Well, its a nice thing to believe anyway.

The disturbing thing—and I have no logical basis for this statement. It's just a vibration I feel. This is going to be the last D.C. good time demonstration. Don't ask me why.

So it was fun. It was also a microcosm of the revolution. It was a confrontation on an intellectual level with the empire we're trying to get rid of, when we smoked dope at the base of the Washington Monument with a couple of hundred cops watching, and later when we skirmished with the police.

It was a confrontation on a personal level when we had to deal with the straights there personally not our cultural struggle first and our relationship to our families second. That part was heavy. It is quite easy to TALK about smashing the state, offing the pigs, and trashing the oppressors, but DOING IT—when you're face to face with "ordinary" solent majority freaks who don't wear cop uniforms and are unarmed is another thing altogether.

I wonder—when faced with this kind of confrontation—how many revolutionaries would stick their thumbs in their mouths and curl up in a mentally foetal position.

I sure don't have the answer to that one, heavy rap fans.

It seems we had the smoke-in after all.

Right and Wrong ripped us off, and the "movement heavies" couldn't get together, so we did what we've always done, from Woodstock to the last Balto-Cong demonstration in May—we just did it ourselves—TOGETHER.

There was no admission, there was no fences, no speeches, no collections, no march routes, and NO fucking marshalls.

People started arriving as early as Thursday and the D.C. free community put them up until The Big Day. Some crashed on the grounds of the Washington Monument on Friday night. Unfortunately they were forced to play a rather unfriendly game of hide and go gas with the local constabulary. I heard they didn't mind it too much though. Matter of fact, some of the people I talked to kind of dug it. Of course, they were stoned when I talked to them.

I arrived at dawn—stoned. There were about three hundred freaks there then—including a large contingent of Yippies who were painting people's faces with orange and blue war paint. I got some of the blue, but none of the orange.

Everyone was sitting on the lawn in front of the Washington Monument smoking them funny looking cigarettes and puffing on pipes. I joined them. Fast.

Was the dope good? Let me put it this way—I took fifteen pictures before I realized I had no film in my camera. Yeah, it was good dope.

By nine o'clock the crowd numbered around a thousand—all stoned. The Billy Graham Honor America Before it Honors You Buddy Day Ceremonies were getting ready at the Lincoln Memorial so I walked over to the area of the press trailer so's I could get press credentials. I was prevented from doing so by a cop.

"I can't even get into the press trailer to see whether I can get credentials?" I said.

"That's right."

"Oh."

I was really stoned.

After an uneventful stroll around the reflecting pool and Lincoln Memorial—well, I did rip off an Amerikan Flag from a vendor and tie it upside down around my arm—I walked back to the Washington Monument grounds and found the number of freaks had almost doubled. Upon visiting the Yippie tent (a large tree) somebody laid a tab of that dynamite white acid on me— FREE! Yippies are like that.

From then on things became a little strange. Let's see—I remember ripping off a vendor for a box of Crackerjax. I remember that.

Well, I trucked on over to the Lincoln Memorial again and found that there were lots of freaks in the reflecting pool. Just then Deliverance Billy and Friends cranked up their Gods and began their show.

There was one disturbance at the Lincoln Memorial end of the pool when the cops used horses to keep the freaks from storming the ceremonies. Couple of people got kicked in the head by the horses.

I got off.

I'm afraid you're going to have to ask your friends about the details of what happened after that because—well, I know what I saw but it's hard to tell how accurate any of this is.

For instance, I don't think the Lincoln Memorial Rally turned into the Reichstag. I mean there really weren't any Nazi flags, were there?

As far as I can figure out, there was some head busting and gassing. This may have been caused by things like the Yippies liberating a giant supermarket opening floodlight, tossing it in the pool and using it as a raft.

By the way there was a huge thunderstorm—high winds, lightning, and lots of rain. We caused that. There was so much fucking freak energy that it directed itself upwards and the fury of the heavens broke loose on Bob Hope's festivities. Well, its a nice thing to believe anyway.

One disturbing thing—and I have no logical basis for this statement. It's just a vibration I felt. This is going to be the last D.C. good time demonstration. Don't ask me why.

So it was fun. It was also a microcosm of the revolution. It was a confrontation on an intellectual level with the empire we're trying to get rid of, when we smoked dope at the base of the Washington Monument with a couple of hundred cops watching, and later when we skirmished with the police.

It was a confrontation on a personal level when we had to deal with the straights there personifying our cultural struggle first and our relationship to our families second. That part was heavy. It is quite easy to TALK about smashing the state, offing the pigs, and trashing the oppressors, but DOING IT—when you're face to face to face with "ordinary" silent majority freaks who don't wear cop uniforms and are unarmed is another thing altogether.

I wonder—when faced with this kind of confrontation—how many revolutionaires would stick their thumbs in their mouths and curl up in a mentally foetal position.

I sure don't have the answer to that one, heavy rap fans.

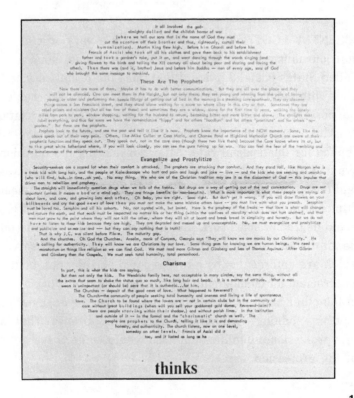

12 Democracy in the Newsroom: Notes on the Movement Towards Non-seigneurial Journalism

By Ron Dorfman

RECENTLY I GOT THE official word from a very official source that journalism is not a profession. The official source is the United States Postal Service. What does the postal service have to do with determining professional qualifications? It has a special postal rate for professional organizations. The Association of Working Press, which publishes the *Chicago Journalism Review*, applied for this special rate. After considering the question for five months, the postal service finally sent its official answer. It said that professional organizations usually require for membership certain minimum educational standards, generally a professional degree of some sort, and a more or less codified body of standards and ethics which the members agree to observe and which are enforceable by a professional certification body. The requirement for membership in the Association of Working Press, on the other hand, is simply that the member be engaged in the reporting, editing, writing or broadcasting of news. That is the only professional qualification most would want to see enforced on the profession.

But there is a real problem here. We like to think of ourselves as professionals. But if we are a profession, we are the only profession that operates exclusively within the framework of a profit-oriented industry. We do not have any licensing authority to say who is and who is not a journalist, what is good journalism and what is not. We want a journalism that will, as Tom Wicker said in the A. J. Liebling Counter-Convention in 1972, "Let a hundred flowers bloom." What he meant was new journalism, old journalism, advocacy journalism, literary journalism—he didn't care what it was as long as it was good journalism. But unfortuately every year there are fewer and fewer flowers—blooming or not. And this is due to the very peculiar organization of our industry. It is at the same time hyper-modern and terribly antiquated. Half of us, it sometimes appears, work in institutions which are part of large and diversified conglomerate corporations. And the other half work in dynastic family enterprises which are really the last bastion in the modern world of the feudal system of primogeniture. There is no inherent contradiction between the practice of professional journalism and the present organization of the industry. But most will recognize the essential truth of the statement that what little good journalism we have in this country is dependent upon the noblesse oblige, or really the whimsy of three individuals, three very rich persons. They are Kay Graham, "Punch" Sulzberger, and Otis Chandler.* That's all there is.

The problem is compounded by the fact that there is really no alternative to giant media institutions. I. F. Stone is often praised for his twenty years of solitary journalism in Washington. But Stone couldn't do what he did unless he had the daily output of the *Washington Post*, *The New York Times*, *Le Monde*, the Associated Press, *The Times* of London, and a few other publications on which to base his dissection of official mendacity. Even exponents of the new alternate media have said they consider their work supplementary—that *The New York Times* is still the

*Katharine Graham, publisher of the *Washington Post*; Arthur Ochs Sulzberger, publisher of *The New York Times*; Otis Chandler, publisher of the *Los Angeles Times*.

primary source of news. They are perfectly right. Yet, we know how imperfect are *The New York Times*, CBS and the *Washington Post*. We know that because they sometimes tell us about each other. Gay Talese tells us about them. And Spiro Agnew told us about them. But how much less perfect then must be the vast majority of the media from which the vast majority of the people in this country get their daily diet of information, opinion and entertainment.

Let me count the ways.

Dorothy Schiff owns the *New York Post*. She has had a monopoly in the afternoon newspaper field in New York ever since the demise of the *World Journal Tribune*, and she is raking in money hand over fist. It is a very profitable operation but she refuses to spend a cent of it to provide anything approximating decent journalism to the 700,000 readers of the *New York Post*. In 1969 there was something of a staff revolt at the *Post* and it ended with a series of meetings which were arranged in the publisher's suite upstairs in the old West Street offices. They were arranged by one of the reporters, a kid fresh out of Harvard whose name is William Woodward III. He is now the publisher of (*more*), the New York journalism review. He is, like Dorothy Schiff, the heir to a large banking fortune and her social equal if not superior. So he was able to arrange these meetings. The requests that the staff made were really very basic. The *New York Post* had one man in its Washington bureau and the staff thought that there ought to be more. Mrs. Shiff said, "Well, we used to have five in the Washington bureau and for one reason or another, over the years we cut that to two and then to one. But you know it really hasn't made any difference." What she meant, of course, was that it had not hurt circulation or revenue. It certainly had made a difference in that newspaper's coverage of Washington. Those meetings were discontinued after a few weeks when Mrs. Schiff found she had unbreakable appointments at the hairdresser.

Eight hundred miles west of New York, in Chicago, there is a young man who is forty years Mrs. Schiff's junior. His name is Marshall Field V. He is young in years but old in heart. He owns two newspapers, the *Chicago Sun-Times* and *Chicago Daily*

News, which, like the *New York Post,* pose as liberal and enlightened spokesmen of the public interest and particularly of the interests of the million and more black people in Chicago and a half million or so Spanish-speaking people in Chicago. But somehow, again very much like the *New York Post* which has never been able to find more than three black reporters for its staff at any one time, the *Sun-Times* and the *Daily News* together have never been able to find more than five or six black reporters at any one time.

Mr. Field has other problems, too. Take advertising for example. Some ads he wants—a lot of ads he wants—but some he doesn't particularly want. He wants ads from supermarkets—what publisher doesn't? When the food editor of the *Sun-Times* and her assistant moved into a new neighborhood and started shopping around in the local supermarkets, they found filthy conditions, mislabeled meats, and other bad conditions. They decided that they ought to say something about those conditions in their food section. So they wrote the next Thursday's food section around that story. The section appeared, as it has to on Thursdays, but that Thursday there was no editorial content in the food section. The staff persisted, however, and the section finally did appear the next week and it had the story in it. The story said that there were these unnamed stores, perhaps, where it was conceivable that there might be found bad conditions, and if the readers ever found any such conditions in their local stores they ought to call it to the attention of the store manager.

On the other hand there is some advertising that Marshall Field doesn't want particularly. For example, the Amalgamated Clothing Workers tried to buy full page ads to explain why they were picketing the Marshall Field & Co. department store. There is very little economic connection between the store and Field Enterprises, which publishes the newspapers. They were picketing because the store was selling imported Italian men's wear and advertising the imported men's wear in the local newspapers. The workers wanted to purchase an ad to explain to the public that they should not buy the men's wear because, they believed, it would cost American textile workers' jobs. Field and the other publisher in town did not want that advertising. In fact, so badly did they not want it that they spent a lot of money on litigation to keep it out of their newspapers.

Well, keep traveling west another 800 miles or so, and you find a newspaper which calls itself the Voice of the Rocky Mountain West—*The Denver Post*. This is another enlightened liberal newspaper which regularly sells its editorial columns to shopping centers and real estate developers. This is exposed every other year in one or another professional forum but the newspaper goes blithely on.

Keep going west and you find the *San Francisco Chronicle*, which retains two law firms in Washington to protect itself against the antitrust laws. But it keeps not a single correspondent in the nation's capital.

The *New York Post* and the *Chicago Sun Times*, the *Denver Post*, and the *San Francisco Chronicle* are not, by far, the worst newspapers in this country but they are embarrassments to the journalists who work for them. Those journalists think that they might and ought to be able to do something a little better.

Reporters have always bitched, generally in bars and to one another. If they were not content with bitching in bars, they would quit and become PR men. The classic slogan was, "Well, if I am going to be a whore, Goddamn it, I might as well be a well-paid whore." Or else they adopted a veneer of cynicism, saying "Everybody is crazy except me and I am just an observer of the passing scene."

In the early 1960's something else began to happen. People began coming out of the universities into journalism, people who had been marked by the characteristic stigmata of this generation. We were indelibly changed by the civil rights movement. We had begun what we now see is a movement, of which Ralph Nader is the highest expression, a movement for institutional responsibility—responsibility to a wider public and more particularly responsibility to the men and women who have to live and work within the institution. But we came to the newsrooms and we saw all the same things that everybody else had always seen in newsrooms and we did the same kind of bitching.

But then came 1968. What happened in 1968 was that reporters suddenly got defined. All sorts of groups in society had been, in the idiom of the day, getting themselves together, which really meant finding collective self-identity. Reporters have always resisted that and have been loners, nonjoiners, and individualists. But all of a sudden in the streets of Chicago in 1968 we found out that wasn't really our option. We were being defined. The police did not care whether any individual reporter was a conservative, a radiclib, apolitical or moderate. As long as he was wearing a press badge he was fair game and the police managed to reach about 75 reporters in the streets of Chicago that week in August. And they touched indirectly every reporter in this country. It was not too long after that that we were further defined by Spiro Agnew and by what became a groundswell of popular discontent with the media and the people who work in it.

After that week in Chicago, when the national press had left, the local newspapers and to a lesser extent the television stations, simply rewrote history, like the Great Soviet Encyclopedia. What had happened that week, suddenly hadn't happened. Over and over again, we got this litany, Mayor Daley's side of the story. The *Chicago Daily News* took the Mayor's official white paper and ran it as an insert. It had a self-mailer on it and you could send it to your out-of-town friends. The paper that I worked for, the *American*, put our television columnist on the front page, attacking the networks for being anti-Chicago—whatever being anti-Chicago is. Those of us who had been in the convention hall and on the streets were very angry. Our own bosses were in effect telling the people that we had lied. There was a lot of phone calling back and forth. Finally, about a hundred of us met in a bar and had several meetings in the course of about a week and a half. Out of those meetings came the *Chicago Journalism Review*. We did not know what to expect. We just knew that we wanted to do something—that what we were most capable of doing was reporting and writing and that was the form our expression should take. That happened in 1968. There are now a dozen other local journalism reviews around the country.

There have been, quite apart from journalism reviews, many

other kinds of activity within the nation's newsrooms that go under the rubric of the reporter's revolt, or the revolution in the newsroom—very grandoise terms. It's nothing of the sort. But what it is, is an attempt to impose from below some sense of professional integrity on the publishers and broadcasters who own and run our news organizations. If we are professionals, we are going to have to be professionals with all that implies. We are not hirelings. Having employed us, the publisher certifies our competence and he must then free us to do the job that we have to do in the way that we best can do it. As Tom Wicker said, "A journalism that places reins and restraints on our work, which cannot cope with men of ideas, intellect and experience, simply cannot publish the best work that reporters are capable of doing."

RON DORFMAN is editor of the Chicago Journalism Review, a publication devoted to reviewing and criticizing the media and which also frequently carries reports which the major media won't. Dorfman helped found the CJR in 1968. Since then the Review has inspired similar efforts in many cities across the nation.

Dorfman is a former reporter with the City News Bureau of Chicago and Chicago's American (now Chicago Today). He covered the Democratic National Convention in Chicago in 1968. He is a graduate of the University of Chicago and was a professional journalism fellow at Stanford University. He is president of the Association of Working Press.

In his article Dorfman discusses the need for and movement toward democracy in the newsroom—that is, an atmosphere in which the journalist is free to function as his training and talents tell him he ought. In Dorfman's view, the journalist is not now free to function in this manner, but rather must do what he is told by various overlords. This situation has led to a much less effective press than we might otherwise have, Dorfman feels.

In addition to pushing within the established media for this liberty, reporters have in recent years begun to produce their own publications. The journalism reviews are the major result of this effort, and the Chicago Journalism Review is perhaps the premier example. In these reviews, the journalists report as their employers in the mass media will not allow them. In fact they frequently criticize the performance of their employers. The following article reprinted from CJR finds the publication doing what many feel it does best—once again taking on the Chicago media.

Editor's Note: As this book was going to press, it was reported that Dorfman had resigned as editor of the Chicago Journalism Review.

13 No Cease-fire in Chicago Press

Chicago Journalism Review, May, 1973

By Neal Rosenau

FROM THE TIME the Paris Agreement was signed January 27 until Nguyen Van Thieu visited the United States in early April, the Chicago newspapers' main contribution to the supposed return to normalcy was a daily diet of news about returning prisoners of war.

The POWs are of little concern here. What is at issue is the role the media play in policy-making and how the Chicago press has filled its oft-stated commitment to peace.

Push aside the patent hype of POWs. What remains in the Chicago press is a sadly unbalanced picture of what's happening in Vietnam and the rest of Indochina. In the balance of stories they print, in the sources they get their information from, and in the interpretation they make of events in headlines and stories, the Chicago papers present a one-sided picture of what's happening in Indochina, and what the U.S. role is there, and what that role ought to be.

There are an alarming number of stories that many Chicagoans never see. Stories of ugly torture and abuse of war prisoners in Saigon's jails. Stories of massive violations of the Peace Agreement by Nguyen Van Thieu's forces. Stories of western newsmen bounced out of Saigon, like drunks out of a bar, when they insulted proprietor Thieu.

On the other hand, there has been a plethora of stories about "Vietcong" or "North Vietnamese" violations of the Agreement, most of them concentrated around the time of General Thieu's visit to the U.S. There was almost nothing to indicate that the "other side" was charging just as many violations against "our side," perhaps with as much validity. And little of what the Chicago papers printed indicated how true any of these charges were.

One example serves here for the moment. On March 17, the *New York Times* reported a charge by the Provisional Revolutionary Government (PRG—Vietcong) that the U.S. was violating the Paris Agreement by sending large shipments of war materials into Saigon. On the same day, Washington charged that Hanoi was sending vast amounts of war supplies down the Ho Chi Minh Trail (a charge later retracted by the State Department). In the spirit of the Paris accord, the *Times* gave both stories equal headlines and equal space.

But in Chicago, the *Daily News*, March 19, advertised the story with one of its typically massive headlines: "BIG RED BUILD-UP PERILS VIET TRUCE." In 27 inches of copy, the *News* said not a word about the PRG's charges or about whether or not their scare banner might be true.

What the Agreements say

The imbalance that becomes apparent in a careful examination of Chicago papers' coverage of the transition from war to peace in Vietnam is particularly disturbing in light of the provisions of the "Agreement on Ending the War and Restoring Peace in Vietnam," signed in Paris January 27.

The Agreement falls into two essential parts, in terms of establishing peace in Vietnam. First, it is the responsibility of the United States to completely withdraw all military personnel and

126

Channel 44: its license was illegal
Studs Terkel: "Agnew is right…"
The Trib: a pitiful, helpless giant

Chicago
Journalism
Review

MAY 1972   VOLUME 5, NUMBER 5   PRICE

Pulling ourselves together in New York

to cease all intervention in the internal affairs of South Vietnam. Specifically, in Article 9, the Agreement says that the U.S. (and other foreign countries) "shall not impose any political tendency or personality on the South Vietnamese people." Secondly, the Agreement recognizes two armies and two administrations in South Vietnam charged jointly with the responsibility to settle the political destiny of the south.

This point is important because, despite this recognition of both the Provisional Revolutionary Government and the Thieu government (Republic of South Vietnam), Washington's consistent attitude has been that the Saigon regime is the "sole legitimate government of South Vietnam" (Nixon, January 23, the night he announced the Agreement).

In hammering out the agreement, Henry Kissinger and Le Duc Tho recognized the two opposing regimes as a reality of South Vietnamese life; as Kissinger said, "It is not easy to achieve through negotiations what has not been achieved on the battlefield." The Agreement was ratified by major nations of the world in a Paris conference in February, recognizing both the PRG and Saigon as legitimate in this transition period. But the official, ex cathedra statements of the Nixon Administration do not.

The Chicago press—ignoring alike the international agreement, the political realities of South Vietnam, the opinion of the world, and the best interests of most Americans, who have wanted peace for half a generation—has taken the Nixon Administration line almost without question.

Take Thomas B. Ross's Washington analysis from the April 4 Sun-Times as an example: "The President was warned by U.S. intelligence in advance of the meeting with Thieu that the North Vietnamese probably will launch another big offensive this month to 'liberate' enough territory to set up a revolutionary government."

In light of the Agreement and of the military situation in South Vietnam, Ross's information is misleading on several grounds:

1. The Provisional Revolutionary Government already exists, recognized internationally and legitimized in the Paris Agree-

ment; it does not have to be "set up." If it has no visible capitol, it is only because its ground-force army has little chance to protect an above-ground capitol from Thieu's air force, the third largest in the world.

2. The PRG and its military arm, the National Liberation Front (NLF) control no major cities, but even the most conservative estimates concede their control of large sections of the countryside. They, themselves, claim nearly all the countryside, leaving only the cities to Saigon control.

3. The fact that the NLF is a large, dedicated force indigenous to South Vietnam is ignored by Ross. It is difficult to tell—impossible for the Chicago papers—to what extent the Democratic Republic of Vietnam (DRV—North Vietnam) controls the NLF, how heavily DRV troops affect the fighting in South Vietnam, or what percentage of NLF weapons come from the north and how many are captured American arms. But it's a fiction to pretend the PRG and NLF don't exist.

It's not surprising that the Nixon Administration, with its record for bellicose policies in Indochina, should refuse to recognize the PRG, even though it signed an Agreement that does so. But it is disturbing that the Chicago press should again get itself into the witless role of doing public relations for the Pentagon and its Saigon proteges.

The key role of the media

It's disturbing and dangerous because of the nature of the Paris Agreement and the role that public opinion must play in its implementation. The Agreement is not a treaty because it was not ratified by the Senate. It didn't have to be. It is an executive agreement, sufficient in this case because the war was never legally a war under the Constitution—it wasn't declared by Congress.

It is a political settlement, based on an assessment of the battlefield situation, world opinion and diplomatic considerations, and the attitude of the press and public in America. It is these same factors that will affect the outcome of the peace and how closely the President adheres to the Paris document.

129

Given Richard Nixon's penchant for promising one thing then doing another (remember "peace is at hand" in October and the blitzkreig in December), one of the major checks on what he might do is that vague, amorphous thing called public opinion. Since the beginning of the Vietnam involvement, one of the major restrictions on White House and Pentagon policy has been a consideration of what public opinion would allow (though not what the public would like). The *Pentagon Papers*, the official Defense Department history of the war, reveal many instances where policies were accepted or rejected on the basis of what public reaction might be.

That's where the media come in. They may not actually lead public opinion, but they can mislead it. What people think is largely based on what information they get from the media. Specifically in this case, what the press does or doesn't report about what is happening in Indochina and about the U.S. Government's activities there will affect what Americans think the U.S. role should be. That opinion, in turn, will have a large effect on how carefully the President must abide by the provisions of the Paris Agreement.

In that light, it's dangerous cant to have the *Daily News* Saigon correspondent Larry Green telling us that "both the press and the public are prisoners of what they are being told" by the Pentagon. That may be the *object* of the Nixon Administration's rules, rantings, and proposed restrictions: to keep covered up any news that does not support its policies. But to have key correspondents willingly crawl into the bottle and hand the cork to the governmental genie is frightening.

In all fairness to Green, he's been able to cut through the Pentagon's propaganda curtain with an astute analysis now and then. But here he's a good example of an attitude of mind that's dangerous and defeatist at a time when reportorial feist and editorial pluck could help make the difference between real peace and real disaster.

How the press has filled its role

What has happened in the last two months is that, by and large, the Chicago papers have presented a rosy picture of the

Saigon regime and the U.S. role in South Vietnam and a sinister picture—or no picture at all—of the "other side," the PRG and Hanoi.

Occasionally, the press has done a good job. On March 4, for instance, the *Sun-Times* made it clear that all is not well in Saigon by running a front page story describing tortures in Thieu's "tiger cages" on Con Son Island. The same edition reported, inside, that there were hundreds of bodies of Saigon prisoners, who were supposed to be released, floating in the sea off Thailand.

But rarely, if ever, do we get a clear picture of life in Saigon-controlled areas of South Vietnam, reports like the one by Thomas W. Lippman in the February 18 *Washington Post: "Thieu is continuing to run South Vietnam almost as if the Paris cease-fire agreement had never been signed, with the army and police as his principal instruments of statecraft. . . ."*

In general, coverage of the Thieu regime has been favorable. There's an occasional mention that the Thieu government has threatened to deport newsmen whose dispatches from South Vietnam are "harmful to the national defense," that is, stories uncomplimentary to the regime or that describe life in PRG-controlled areas. Reporters from other cities and from wire services have been expelled from South Vietnam (Donald A. Davis, acting bureau chief of UPI in Saigon was ordered to leave March 4, according to the *New York Times*). But no Chicago newsmen have been ordered out, and public concern in the press here is low.

Even the prisoners held by Saigon, estimated by some to number 200,000—and the subject of considerable research by such groups as the American Friends Service Committee, the Indochina Resource Center in Washington, and Don Luce's Indochina Mobile Education Project—have received little attention in the Chicago media. The press has virtually ignored the question, even when it was brought to their own doorstep.

On March 9, two French citizens, schoolteachers Jean Pierre Debris and Andre Menras, recounted their own experiences in Thieu's jails at a Chicago press conference. Three of the Loop dailies ran a story about them, each a short notice and far back in the paper. The *Daily News* said nothing about them. Only the weekly *Chicago Express* gave them a forum to relate their experience, in a report by Fred Melcher.

Nguyen Van Thieu, who by the weight of objective evidence ranks as an unquestioned dictator, has gotten a most favorable reaction from the Chicago press. His trip to the U.S. in early April got the press reaction it was designed for. Thieu's picture appeared daily in the *Tribune*. The *Daily News* Insight column remarked at length on the "New Thieu." The *Sun-Times'* Thomas B. Ross found him to be a crafty, effective politician; this despite Ross's earlier report (April 5) that Thieu plans to disrupt and delay the Agreement's provisions for political solution in South Vietnam for at least a year.

Thieu's trip was neatly preceded in the press by several days of charges that North Vietnam was shipping massive supplies down the Ho Chi Minh Trail. These charges may be a prelude to American reintervention, as some commentators, including *Newsweek* (March 28), have speculated, or they could be used as arguments for continued and increased American aid to the Thieu regime.

Whatever the reason, these stories weren't without purpose, as Larry Green noted on March 20: "The American public is being prepared for something," he said, though he couldn't say what. He cautioned "that in the past there was frequently little correlation between reality and what was said officially about conditions and events in Indochina."

If Green knew this, or if the *Daily News* editors shared his concern, they didn't show it. Green clearly makes sense sometimes, when he's allowed to analyze the situation in Vietnam. But the *Daily News* has been a prime example of unbalanced reporting. Green's reports of cease-fire violations invariably quote "intelligence sources" in Saigon and are filled to capacity with "reportedlies." In normal conditions that may be no great fault, since any journalist does his share of hack jobs rewriting press releases. But Green's share comes from Saigon and U.S. military sources, and his dispatches form a weight in the balance between war and peace.

Comparing the volume of copy space expended on charges

and countercharges about atrocities or violations of the Agreement in the *Daily News* during two weeks from March 8 to 21, researchers for the *Indochina Bulletin* found six column inches "against Saigon" and 127 inches "against the PRG or Hanoi." (The *Bulletin* is a national monthly anti-war newspaper, formerly called the *War Bulletin*. The Midwest edition, published in Chicago, is distributed free by volunteers.)

Headlines on the *Daily News* stories in the same period were even more interesting: three square inches against Saigon, 165 square inches against the PRG and Hanoi. The latter included such banners as REDS POUR TROOPS INTO S. VIET. (The impact of that headline was, perhaps, matched only by the one January 26: CONG MAP NEW GUERRILLA TERROR.)

The figures on *Daily News* balance are significant not only because of Green's own reservations but also in light of the admission by a U.S. official in Saigon who told *Newsweek* [*March 28*], "*I would guess that the South Vietnamese* [Saigon] *have accounted for 60 per cent or more of the cease fire violations.*" Gary Porter, a Vietnam scholar from Cornell University, described how U.S. charges of massive infiltration from North to South Vietnam were questionable at best. His article, which appeared in the Cornell *Daily Sun* March 20, noted that, on the basis of the "intelligence reports" themselves, the alleged infiltration may have taken place before the cease-fire went into effect—in other words, during the same period that the United States was shipping "more than 600 aircraft, among other things" into Saigon.

Washington eventually revised its accusations (*Daily News*, March 31) but the charges, emblazoned in bold type, had already had their effect. And the headline on Green's "Insight" article April 6 did little to clear the air: "THREATS TO PEACE MOUNT," it said under the subscript, "Evidence of Red infiltration into South collected by planes, sensors, humans."

Green tried to make sense of conflicting statistics from "the most reliable intelligence sources." The 15,000 troops that allegedly infiltrated since January 27 had been en route before that date, their numbers more than offset by the 16,000 troops that Saigon claims to have killed since the Agreement was signed.

(This may be some indication of who's doing the shooting.)

The most significant aspect of Green's analysis is his revelation, far down in the story, that most of the infiltrators moving from north to south now are "political organizers" and "former southerners who went north in 1954" at the time of the Geneva Agreements. Contrary to the headline on his article, Green said this indicates that "the Communists plan for a political struggle," something a resumption of large-scale war would preclude.

Green also said that Hanoi and the PRG are hauling in artillery and troops, but the evidence he cites makes it look as if war is a contingency only if political struggle becomes impossible.

As regards the PRG and its legally equal status with the Saigon government in South Vietnam, the Chicago papers have almost totally ignored it. The PRG and NLF remain the "Vietcong," "VC," or "Cong," terms as derogatory as they are inaccurate.

But nomenclature aside, little or nothing in the Chicago press has indicated their importance as a force in South Vietnam. The *Los Angeles Times*, February 2, and the *New York Times*, April 4, each carried stories by correspondents who entered PRG areas to find out what life there was like. The *New York Times* story was less complimentary than the one from L.A., but that matters little; both papers recognized the existence of the other force in South Vietnam and tried to make it real for Americans. The *Sun-Times* gets the *Los Angeles Times* service and the *Tribune* gets the *New York Times* service. but neither story appeared in Chicago.

What it all means

There is little question that the Nixon Administration and the Thieu regime are making it difficult for western journalists to ferret out news that contradicts their official line. Thieu has expelled journalists from South Vietnam. Reporters are being harassed in the U.S. and in Indochina. Newspapers that get too nosey, like the *Washington Post*, have been hounded by the Administration. The prosecution in the *Pentagon Papers* trial is attempting to make classified documents into private government

134

property, and the Nixon Administration has introduced legislation to the same effect.

The list of impositions or threats on press freedom could extend for pages. But journalists, from publishers on down, know them. They should be an indication that something strange is going on and that journalists can't accept the Executive's word as fact.

Granted, too, it's sometimes difficult to separate the truth from the fabrication when dealing with the well-trained, well-heeled, and experienced information-makers of Washington or Saigon. They've been at the game a long time. In Vietnam, the PR war has been going on since the 50s. In 1955, the Pentagon was bragging that it had cultivated a group of sympathetic reporters who were very helpful in promoting the U.S. government line to the American public (*Pentagon Papers*, Gravel Edition, vol. I, p. 581).

That this sort of thing is still happening is clear from the report of the massacre of "250 to 500 Vietnamese officials" last summer when North Vietnamese troops controlled large sections of Binh Dinh Province. Former *New York Times* correspondent Thomas C. Fox, now working with Dispatch News Agency, wrote that investigations by Western journalists in Saigon after the *New York Times* published the massacre story have revealed the following:

"—All Government evidence for the execution and imprisonment charges have been traced back to C.I.A. documents of Vietnamese military refugee interrogations.

"—Several of the documents, including one attesting to 100 of the 250 alleged executions, are based on hearsay refugee evidence, not on firsthand eyewitness accounts.

"—Some Binh Dinh American intelligence officers have speculated the C.I.A. papers are 'exaggerated.'

"—American officials in Saigon and Washington have deliberately waged a campaign to maximize the public impact of the alleged killings and have distorted facts to do so."

Fox's report appeared in *American Report*, a weekly newspaper published by Clergy and Laity Concerned, on September 15. No Chicago paper reported his findings.

Examples like this indicate that the information machines, far from being turned off, are still rolling full force. And Tom Fox's example is proof that hard-nosed investigation can still turn up the facts—or at least discount the propaganda.

Unless they wish to become a mere pipeline for official government information, the media owe it to themselves to investigate and to report news that contradicts Washington (maybe even print news from Gai Phon, the PRG's official press service, it may be no more accurate than the Pentagon, but it may be no less), and challenge the White House when it's necessary.

But more than media self-interest is at stake here. The whole question of American involvement in Vietnam—and in Cambodia and Laos—is still at issue. The Paris Agreement only outlined the next stage of affairs in Vietnam. It clearly hasn't affected what's happening in Cambodia, and we desperately need information on who's fighting whom there and what, exactly, the U.S. role is in the "Khmer Republic." It should be clear by now that the nature of things in South Vietnam is sadly wanting for effective coverage.

It's obvious, too, that the Nixon Administration is determined yet to tie the United States to reactionary regimes throughout Indochina. But it should be the American public—not the President and not the press—who should decide whether the communist bogeymen in Vietnam, Laos, and Cambodia are all that threatening to what Americans want in their lives, and whether the battle in Indochina is worth the continued cost. The press's job is to make sure they get the information they need to decide.

And if the Chicago editors really believe what they say in their editorials about peace, it's time they reread the Paris Agreement and start reporting what America and its allies are doing to make it work.

Hanoi has bombers, ships, and mines hanging over its head to keep it honest. Nixon has only us.

(*Neal Rosenau is a Chicago free-lance writer. He has been a reporter for newspapers in California and Illinois, and taught his-*
136

tory at Roosevelt University. His work appears regularly in the Chicago Express. He was assisted in research for this article by Fred Melcher and Steve Packard.)

14 | Editorial Control in the Newsroom

By Ernest Imhoff

ONE OF THE REASONS I am a newspaperman today is my first editor, a guy named Phil Lee who ran the city room of a New England newspaper fifteen years ago when I started working as a darkroom errand boy. Phil Lee would not like much of today's journalism, I am afraid—especially the chest beating and self-consciousness and the humorlessness of some of it. In those days Phil didn't have to beat off too many activist reporters or concern himself greatly with participatory journalism. He was a quiet, firm guy who had the idea that reporters and editors should gather the news and leave the sloganeering to the politicians, the crooks and the do-gooders outside the building. As for the highly personalized writing of people like Damon Runyon or Gene Fowler of an earlier day, Phil was probably glad that their 1920's and 1930's version of the New Journalism had come and gone.

The closest thing on that paper to an activist reporter was a fellow who wanted badly to write about how upset he was over the latest outrage. When this guy wrote straight he was very good. But Phil Lee always said no when he tried to work his opinions into the news columns. The frustrated writer finally devised an answer. He began writing letters to the editor as well as writing straight news. Some of those letters were fairly interesting. They usually concerned banning the bomb or protecting our milk or a similar 1950's issue. But the ground rules were that no letters were published on any subject that he was covering in the news columns for Phil Lee. Remain detached was the idea.

There are always subjective judgments in the news business on what stories get printed, what stories get killed, what goes in or what is left out of printed stories, how things are worded, how stories are played in the paper, whether to give a story a one-column headline and what page to put it on, but the reporter shouldn't take that quantum jump and begin to tell the reader what's wrong with the world. It may be necessary to give the reader background and analysis and interpretation, but mainly give him facts so he can make up his own mind. Readers are not dummies, although most writers and editors at one time or another have thought so. Look down on the reader and the editor and the reporter are dead. The practice of balanced reporting and fairness is what I recall most about Phil Lee.

The importance of this kind of reporting was drilled home to me when I covered the great sewage debate for his paper. It was the big story there for about a year and a half. Before it was over, I had written sixty or seventy stories. The federal government told this town and others to clean up their rivers. Indeed, the rivers were dirty. The local administration began pushing the open lagoon system for sewage disposal saying it was nice and it was cheap. As a backup, the town fathers supported a conventional sewage treatment plant. The opponents to this said take your lagoons and sewage plants elsewhere.

A third group, and there were a lot of people in that group, just didn't know what was going on. With a nudge from my city room and some curious readers, I began digging more into the lagoon alternatives. Who needs a sewage plant in a town of 7,000? What is the matter with a straight system? Won't those ponds smell up the place? How about a chance of cost overruns on those figures? It took a lot of digging. In retrospect, I should have done more. But the experience strikes me as important. It shows straight journalism trying to be fair, searching out the other person's side, overlooking any lack of eloquence, looking skeptically at official versions, looking skeptically at everyone, digging for material not readily available but important, and remembering that a paper has a duty in its news columns to try to let the readers make up their own minds. The lagoons lost in this town; the status quo lost and the town built a conventional sewage plant. Had the paper become an open advocate instead of attempting to provide full and fair coverage, it would not have been doing its job. This is one reason why I believe in straight journalism. There are others.

In a small city, well-covered by a daily, people pound on your door, people call you at all hours, people stop you on the street and poke their fingers deep into your shoulders and people want to keep buying you a cup of coffee. You get reactions. A lot of them. You understand a little bit about how people are thinking and how they are reacting to things. In a metropolitan daily, the reporter may well be isolated to some extent—not from the news sources since they are always interested in talking, but from the readers, the people for whom the paper should be written and edited. You can go for days with a series and maybe get a few phone calls and a letter to the editor. Five letters on one subject is a really big deal. I miss hearing more reactions because I wish I knew more about my readers. I like to think that I am working for them, not the politicians, not the noisemakers, not the do-gooders.

Newspaper readers are a faceless audience or even rubber-faced, more divergent than the readership of *Playboy, Time, Cosmopolitan* or such other specialized publications. But we do know some things about the readership of a general circulation newspaper. For instance, readers read an afternoon paper toward the end of the day, when they may be tired, and they spend twenty to forty minutes on it. They read sports, comics, national news, and local news. They jump around. They get turned on by television. They may not read the newspaper every day. They throw the paper away the next day. Most buy just one daily newspaper. If they are going to get some local news, it is going to be there, at least if it is printed. It is not going to be in any other paper. And here is the point. As an editor I have to try to put out a fair and balanced paper for these faceless readers. And with twenty-five, thirty or forty reporters, with four major deadlines a day, with thirty-five columns of local news space, with more story ideas than we can ever assign, with stories running longer than they should, with important stories not being covered, with different ideas circulating on what should be covered, an editor must exercise some control in the newsroom to achieve this goal.

Reporters collectively exercising editorial powers is a system that can't work well. Committees make lousy editors. But reporters having access to editors—I am for this completely. At the *Evening Sun*, we have three assistant city editors and we are always open and available to reporters. We are very much interested in reporters' opinions and their suggestions. At one point or another, however, someone has to make a decision and that decision cannot be made by nine people voting.

Another topic of concern in this new era is reporters' and editors' involvement in politics outside the newsroom. I am against this. Who would believe the printed words of a daytime skeptical reporter who waves a flag at night? I think the believability of the person as a reporter and the paper's believability would be diminished.

The New Journalism is indeed a circus with many side shows. Some of them are good and some of them are bad. (Personally, I wish there were more clowns in the show.) Thus far, I have tried to indicate some of the problems of these side shows. A great danger of the New Journalism, however, lies in the fact that a concern with the side shows may lead journalists to forget the basics of good journalism, which ought to be a part of old or new journalism. I have my own little list of journalistic sins which anyone who claims to be a competent journalist ought to consider.

First, consider the practice of sandbagging people by anonymous criticism. The good reporter should avoid critics in shadows. This is where the writer names a person charged with something unfavorable and does not name the critic. This might happen for a number of reasons. Maybe the reporter thinks he cannot get the story if he violates the confidential source. Or someone says, "Look, I really got something great here but don't use me as a critic." This is acceptable if the reporter uses this as a tip and goes on from there to other sources. People will try to go off the record to grind their axes. They give you a juicy tidbit and then they will say, this is off the record. For the most part I would refuse to go off the record. When the reporter accepts this kind of information, it becomes too easy to blast a person and attribute it to some anonymous source. The reporter is being used and is also not very believable. Readers are discriminating. Talk is very cheap. Print should be a little bit tougher to come by if only because its harmful effects can last a lot longer.

A second sin is angle shooting a story. This is where the editor and reporter start an assignment with a conclusion. The reporter should attempt to control his hangups when pursuing a story. Human nature dictates the reporter will begin to cover a story with opinions. It is natural. But when out on an assignment, the reporter should develop the story with an open mind. Some of the things he may learn are contradictory. But he shouldn't throw out the stuff he personally doesn't believe.

Another little sin, which is as much the fault of editors as reporters, is something called hitting and running. It is important to try to follow up stories. Editors and reporters often move from one subject to another as though they were bar hopping. Their defense is they don't have time or space or interest to follow up an old story, but any one story or series is never the last word. It may be the last printed word for a while but not the complete story. I would guarantee that looking through any newspaper library for the past year would produce clippings of dozens of stories that have been left hanging. Readers therefore have been left hanging, not told what really happened, what the next step was.

Another little problem is ignoring the readers. The reporter should keep the faceless readers in mind when he sits at the typewriter. He may have spent ten hours as a reporter untangling a city budget problem, but remember the reader has not spent ten seconds until he starts to read the lead. So he needs a direct explanation. He needs clear, concise writing. The reporter must

142

anticipate what questions the reader may have at the end of the story, if indeed he ever gets that far. That doesn't mean being afraid to annoy him, that doesn't mean looking down on lower creatures, that doesn't mean foisting the reporter's biases on them, that doesn't mean writing solely for the newsroom crowd, your news sources and your reputation. It means writing and editing so as many readers as possible will understand a tiny bit more about their surroundings.

Number five is minimizing detail. Readers are great at spotting the big little mistake even if they were not at the scene of the action, at the fire, the council meeting or some political blowup. Finding that mistake, they may say "to hell with the whole story. I don't believe it." This can happen if the writer messes up the address of the proposed zoning change, fouls up the number of injuries in a fire and, of course, misspells a person's name. Even if he avoided thirty-two other ways of going wrong and gave a fair account of things, some reader will still see a little mistake. And, then, he will dismiss a thirty paragraph story without thinking twice about it. Perhaps it's unfair but readers do that. After putting down a dime, they can believe whatever they want to believe.

The sixth sin is not knowing enough about what you are writing about although you think you do. Before you as a police reporter decide that cops are brutal or cops are persecuted, at least learn to use some basic tools such as police reports and blotters. Before you begin bitching about a person's rights when arrested, at least know the rights. Before you decide, as a civil liberty specialist or a crime reporter, that the gun law should be more restrictive or less restrictive, at least get to know what the gun law says and what is required of persons who want a permit to carry a handgun. Before you as a court reporter are certain the courts are full of incompetence or that the courts represent the purest form of government service, at least learn something about the way the courts work. The point is do your homework. Learn what is going on. Opinions are a dime a dozen; what is needed is informed knowledgeable reporting.

So those are my favorite little sins of newspapering. Where

the New Journalists are comfortable with the sins, I reject the New Journalism; where the New Journalism disputes them, I welcome it.

ERNEST IMHOFF speaks on the other side of the question of control in the newsroom—the editor's side. As former city editor and current assistant managing editor of the Baltimore Evening Sun he writes as one who has had the responsibility for ensuring that a major metropolitan newspaper is produced daily.

This experience leads him to believe that total democracy in the newsroom will not work. Or as he puts it, "Committees make lousy editors." Someone in the newsroom has to be able to make quick decisions—deadline decisions. Totally democratic proceedings cannot provide for this situation. Additionally, Imhoff believes, someone has to keep in mind the audience for which the paper is published—the faceless, "rubber faced" audience. The editor must ensure that the needs of this total audience are considered and filled.

Before coming to the Sun in 1963, Imhoff worked for the North Adams (Massachusetts) Transcript and the Middletown (Connecticut) Press. He is a graduate of Williams College and the Columbia University Graduate School of Journalism.

15 | Personal Journalism in Television

By Theodore F. Koop

ANY ATTEMPT TO ADAPT personal journalism as espoused by the New Journalists to television cannot work. Television news must, for a variety of reasons, adhere to basic journalistic principles: accuracy, objectivity and impersonal presentation.

Bill Small, Washington vice president of CBS News, wrote in his book, *To Kill a Messenger,* that the so-called New Journalists would encourage an editor to cut his raw material to fit the mold of his prejudices. This is not really a new idea. The penny presses of the earliest days of this country were full of bias and opinion. Anybody with a printing press and a prejudice could put out a paper. Those publishers would admit to printing the little news they had and filling the rest with their opinions. Thomas Jefferson, despite his adherence to the concept of a free press, noted that "the most truthful part of a newspaper is the advertisements."

Small continues, "So the new journalism is really the old journalism. Perhaps it is a mix of those revolutionary era opinionated polemics, and the spirit of the yellow journalism of the early part of this century. It is the latter in the sense that current use of

145

profanity and/or lurid themes and sex or politics is the equivalent of the sensationalism of early Hearst and Pulitzer. It is shock and titillate journalism."*

Eric Sevareid of CBS News said in a speech to the Elmer Davis Foundation a couple of years ago, "Those who would improve our practices in questionable ways come not only from the outside in the form of powerful politicians. Some come from the inside. Militant young men and women in both newspapers and broadcasting, who argue that even the quest for objectivity is a myth, that the prime purpose of the press is not to report the world but to reform it, and in the direction of their ideas. We have all read the learned articles that tell us objective news accounts in the hard news columns or broadcasts tend merely to deceive the reader or hearer, obscure inner truths that the reporter perceives. He must therefore personalize the hard news— infuse it with its own truth. They would not leave this to the editorial writer, columnist and commentator whose work is clearly marked away from the hard news. They believe it will give a true intregity to news columns and news broadcasters." Sevareid concludes, "I believe it will ruin them."

In any consideration of the problems of television news, or of the whole television industry, one must start with three "facts of life." The first "fact of life" is that television is a mass medium, the only truly mass medium in the United States. Newspapers with a million circulation are the unusual rather than the norm. There are no national newspapers in this country as there are in England, which has a small, homogeneous society. Our magazines are limited in circulation, even though they have national scope. But network television talks in terms of audiences of fifty million, seventy-five million or even a hundred million people. A few years ago in a Federal Communications Commission hearing a television network executive was on the stand, and Newton Minow, the FCC chairman, said that he wanted to digress to compliment the network on a recent documentary. He inquired how many people had seen that documentary. The television executive

*William Small, *To Kill A Messenger*, Hastings House, Publishers, Inc., New York, 1970, pg. 288. Reprinted by permission.

replied, "Only seven million." And Minow said, "Only seven million? I think seven million is a tremendous audience for a documentary." But in network terms, seven million is a small audience.

The second "fact of life" is that broadcasting in the United States is by law and by design a commercial institution. Ever since passage of the Communications Act of 1934, which is the charter of broadcasting in the United States, there has never been any serious concentrated effort to change this commercial system. There are some who don't like it. But it is, even in spite of current criticism, generally accepted as the best method for the country.

The third "fact of life," of course, is that radio and television are regulated by the government.

Most people in the United States report that television is their first source of news. It is trite but certainly true to say that television has tremendous impact. It brings the world immediately before you. It is new. It is innovative. It is changing all the time because its technology is changing all the time. The things that the engineers and inventors say will be possible in the next decade boggle the imagination. Who would have thought a decade ago that we could by satellite pick up live television from China?

Television news has reached finally a stage of professionalism of which it can be proud. It was not always thus. When I came into CBS in 1948, television news was really just starting. I remember one day the New York office phoned me and said, "We have some very fine film from Greece. Can't you dig up some kind of story about Greece, either from the State Department or the Embassy, that we can use the pictures with." That sort of thing no longer happens. The pictures fit the news and not vice-versa.

At the outset, no one in television management felt that trained newsmen were necessary to present the news. Pretty boys stood or sat before a camera and in their mellifluous voices intoned material that had either been taken directly off the AP or UPI wires or had been re-written by a $50-a-week employee in the back room. These men on the air were regarded as talent just as

147

actors were. And consequently they were paid tremendous fees as talent.

A television news broadcast, even though it may be spoken by one man, is not solely his work by any means. If he has put in eight man-hours on it, perhaps 100 other people have put in eight man-hours on the same broadcast. So it is actually a team operation, and that is only one reason why it must always be under the control of the news executives. That is also why it would be impractical as well as difficult to permit personal journalism on the air.

Television does, however, have highly personalized journalism. Very few readers can recall what bylines they read in the morning paper, but most are well aware of and consider as individuals and perhaps even as friends, the men and women who appear on the television screen. They come into the living room as guests, and people begin to speak of them as Walter and Chet and David because they feel they know them so well. And so whatever they have to say becomes their own thoughts, their own views in the minds of a great many people. Ed Murrow used to be very cognizant of the power of television, which he said scared him. He felt he was doing his best job when he got criticism from both sides, which did not happen infrequently. Television is also highly personalized journalism because so much of it is alive, and the reporter becomes even more the key to the operation.

Richard Salant, president of CBS News, speaking to the American Society of Newspaper Editors, contrasted the problems of news management in television with those of a newspaper. He said, "You, you the editors, have that most enviable luxury of being able to see all laid out in black and white, each piece prepared by your reporters and rewrite men. You can rewrite, you can transpose words and paragraphs, and you can change words and sentences. As a general rule, we cannot. We can cut a film piece by deletion at the top or bottom and sometimes even in the middle. But we cannot rewrite or rearrange it. And we don't even have that freedom of limited editing when, as we often do, we have to switch for a live piece or take in a film piece from outside New York and include it in our news broadcast. Often we have to

148

substitute prayer for blue pencil. Nor can we really have a good hard look at the make-up of our pages before we hit the streets. The first time we can really get a final hard impression of our news broadcast is when we actually watch it as it goes on the air. Therefore, broadcast news is uniquely marked by great delegation. Real editing controls very often are simply post audit. And so a great deal of reliance must be placed on reporters and producers. There cannot be much on the job training for our reporters."

And that explains very succinctly why television newsmen have to be the most professional that can possibly be obtained, because they have the great responsibility when they are on the air live of reaching the audience with accurate and objective material. They are human beings, of course, and sometimes even the best of them lapse.

It has become commonplace for people to proclaim bias in the news media. Basically people are reading their own biases into television news. A friend of mine, a lawyer in Washington, sincerely believes that every morning in the CBS headquarters in New York, Mr. William Paley, the chairman of the board of CBS, and Dr. Frank Stanton, the vice-chairman, sit down and decide on the newsline that day. And there is nothing that I can say to dissuade him from that view. They are both busy men, and the last thing in the world that they would want to do is to take such a job upon themselves. Walter Cronkite said recently, "I can testify that the executives of my network are less meddlesome in the news process than the publishers for whom I have worked."

When I talk about television news being objective, that it is as impartial as it possibly can be, I am not referring to commentary or editorials on the air. These fields certainly have a very important place, provided they are properly labeled and distinguished from hard news. This is a very important adjunct to the operation of the newsmen themselves. Many radio and television stations are editorializing more and more, but not enough. Every station should editorialize and editorialize much more strongly than some are doing today. Only when the industry becomes very

149

aggressive in that field will its influence be really felt throughout the United States.

Documentaries, of course, have their own place in the television news scheme of things. But the same principles of professional journalism must apply. There must be honesty in reporting, accuracy in reporting, and fairness and objectivity. Here again television gets criticism, perhaps even more than it does in the hard news field. A documentary does frequently take a point of view—even though it tries to acknowledge and explain that there are other points of view on the same subject.

Recall the uproar that was caused by the CBS News documentary, "The Selling of the Pentagon." The critics of the program, instead of attacking the substance, which was somewhat critical of the public relations activities of the military, attacked the editing. I don't know how many hours of raw film were available for the producers to edit into one hour of film—certainly a great many hours. If that raw film were turned over to a random group of editors, each one would come up with a slightly different version of the final documentary. Everyone would pick out different pieces of film, and who can be the final judge as to which one is right and which one, if any, is wrong? The only judgment that can be made is a professional one, and that is whether the producers, the editors, the broadcasters, the reporters have done the best professional job of which they are capable.

Access is another concern proponents of New Journalism in television often raise. Access to a television station is the responsibility of the station management, just as access to the columns of a newspaper is the responsibility of the newspaper ownership. Any other way will lead to chaos. Someone must make a final judgment, a final decision on everything that goes on the air. Who else can make it except the man or the men accountable to the Federal Communications Commission for their license? Here again, if a station does an objective job, a fair job, a journalistic job, a professional job, it is bound to succeed, because it will recognize the diversity of views and interests among the American people. It will present a spectrum of programing, bearing in mind that it still is a mass medium, and cannot give every small

150

group of people the amount of time and the freedom that it would desire.

We must have confidence in the American media system and in the commercial broadcasting system that has been set up by Congress. It does not mean that listeners and viewers should not be vocal. Criticism is very important. But we have many voices in the United States these days. Think only of the several thousand radio stations which exist here. We have so many voices that I think everyone is going to get a chance to have his viewpoint presented somewhere.

Is there a place in the broadcast media for the New Journalism? No, according to THEODORE KOOP, at least not in broadcast news operations. Koop, former vice president for CBS News, Washington, believes that personal journalism, because of the nature of broadcasting, cannot work in that medium.

Among the factors which Koop believes preclude personal journalism in broadcasting are 1) it is government regulated, 2) it is a commercial operation, and 3) it is the only truly mass medium. To serve this mass audience properly the broadcast journalist must be the most professional, the fairest, the most objective reporter available. Broadcast journalism is personalized in the sense that the reporter often becomes a personality; but personal journalism it is not.

Koop joined CBS News in 1948. Prior to that he was a reporter and editor with the Associated Press. During World War II he served in the United States Office of Censorship. He is a graduate of Iowa University. Koop is currently director of the Washington office of the Radio Television News Directors Association.

16 Network Television and the Personal Documentary

From *Film Comment*, Spring, 1970

By Arthur Barron

EVERY TUESDAY NIGHT from 10 to 11 p.m., Eastern Standard Time, the Columbia Broadcasting System television network presents a series of broadcasts called "The CBS Newshour." This program is a direct descendant of "See It Now" and "CBS Reports," the remarkable documentary series of the late 1950's and the early 1960's, produced by the team of Ed Murrow and Fred Friendly. They gave us "Harvest of Shame," "The Population Explosion," and many other documentaries of an hour in length, bearing on the pressing issues of today. It is an hour of blessed reality in an otherwise dreary schedule of fantasy and escapism. CBS is proud of this weekly series, and, in some respects, it should be. It is the only regularly scheduled nighttime, prime-time, documentary series on the air today.*

CBS spends an average of $120,000 for each of these documentary films, and the producers are given as much time as they need to finish them. I have been working on "The Great American Novel" series of three films for a little over a year. That is a lush

---

*This series is no longer seen regularly. See the note on page 159 for an explanation.

working schedule. These films, although they attract shamefully small audiences by "I Love Lucy" standards, nevertheless are an important factor in mass-media communication because, though small by advertising standards, the audiences are vast. Seven and one-half million people, on an average, see these films. . . .

Some of the films are quite worthy—because of their inventiveness, as in "The Italians," the film based on the Barzini book; for their candor, as in Morley Safer's "Vietnam"; for their beauty, as in "Gauguin in Tahiti"; for their balance and objectivity, as in "The Homosexuals"; or for their cinematic technique, as in "The Anderson Platoon," a very beautiful film made in Vietnam which, happily, won the Oscar for documentary films this year.

These films of distinction, however, are rarely ever noteworthy for their boldness. No matter how newsworthy or important, certain subjects never seem to get done on the "CBS Newshour"; nor on any other network for that matter. To the best of my knowledge, network television has never presented a film on the FBI, or on the military-industrial complex, or on Congressional ethics, or on any of a number of other lurid subjects and sacred cows. But the timidity of television in its role as a pillar of the establishment is another subject, and for another time.

Instead, consider . . . the list of programs that actually did make it on the air during the 1966-67 season on the "CBS Newshour." There were forty-eight films in all. Of that number, eleven, the largest single category, dealt with Vietnam—films like "The Letters of Ho Chi Minh" and "Westmoreland on Vietnam." Six of the films dealt with other foreign affairs issues—"How Israel Won the War," "Inside Red China" and "Harvest of Mercy," a film about famine in India. Eight of the films dealt with domestic social problems other than race—problems like air pollution, the hippies, prison, labor and so forth. Four films dealt specifically with race—films like "The Tenement" and "Can We Prevent Tomorrow's Riots Today?" Six films dealt with politics—"Young Mr. Eisenhower," "The Warren Report," "Robert F. Kennedy," and an incredibly moldy fig called "What Happened to Alf Landon?" Two films, "Inside Pot—The Rock Revolution" and "Gauguin in Tahiti," dealt with the arts. Four films persisted in following the test format, with diminishing returns. We had "The National Driver's Test," "The National Science Test," "The National Current Events Test" and "The National Sports and Physical Fitness Test," which I flunked. Finally, there were seven films on miscellaneous subjects—Scotland, Billy Graham, the "brain drain," to name a few.

Now, something that strikes me immediately about this list is that virtually all of the films represent only one tradition of documentary films—the tradition of reportage, of journalism. If you examine this list of films you will find that, almost without exception, all are news documentaries. This emphasis on news, on reportage, is not exclusive to CBS. It is true of all the commercial networks. It is true also of National Educational Television. It is also true of the new Public Broadcast Laboratory, and it is true of the local and independent stations around the country. In television, the documentary of reportage dominates.

Now, . . . [everyone] has seen such films—some are better, some worse—but they share the same characteristics: They are all about war, peace, drug addiction issues. They are all topical, they are all filled with facts, and they are all peopled with experts and authorities, suitably identified with tele-identifications like "LeRoi Jones, poet and militant." They are word-logic issues. Play the soundtrack without the picture and you will still understand the point of the film. Indeed, the pictures are often there merely to illustrate the words. They are very often radio scripts with pictures. "How can we make that complex thought visual," the producer ponders. Sometimes these films are partisan, and there is a narrator to read the words—usually a network correspondent. Controversy is often aired in these films, and controversy often surrounds them when they are shown, . . . [such as in] my films, "Sixteen in Webster Groves" and its sequel "Webster Groves Revisited." . . . Webster is one of eight American cities I can no longer enter.

But if the networks explore controversy, it must be balanced. . . . If a film is about Naziism and they have an anti-Nazi speaking, then they must have Martin Bormann speak. . . . If I were to make

154

a film with Anne Frank, presumably Adolf Hitler would have to have his say, too.

So the news documentaries are balanced, and they tend to be objective too, not merely in the sense of being fair, but cinematically objective. One is quite aware in watching these films that the filmmaker, in this case CBS, is not inside the film, not really in it and with it, but is outside, observing and recording the events, not living through them. CBS is using these films as a forum for the presentation of ideas—always, always keeping its cool, always keeping order, always ready to evaluate, instruct and interpret. CBS is not grooving with the film. It is, as I have said, objective and somehow above it all.

And, finally, all these films have a common purpose: to inform, to instruct. It is a purpose that sees films as politically useful, and it is based on political theory—the Jeffersonian idea of the market place of ideas, and the role of an informed electorate; the Walter Lippmann notion that events are moving so rapidly, and the issues are so complex, that democracy is doomed unless the public is informed. In the ICBM age, what you don't know can kill you. Our job is to see that you know. So films are knowledge, and knowledge is the cement of society. Lenin's notion, too, was that film is the most powerful weapon in the hands of the masses because it can create a revolutionary consciousness and rip the veil from the face of fantasy. Film can become an instrument of class struggle.

This, then, is the theory underlying the news documentary: the belief that the documentary film's supreme function is in energizing, motivating and informing the masses by rendering the complex issues of the day understandable and meaningful. If anyone wanted to, they could trace the history of the news documentary and clearly demonstrate the continuity of that doctrine in this context. One could see the progression of names and titles: Lumiere, Pudovkin, Eisenstein, Grierson and the British school, the "March of Time," Pathe News, the Office of War Information, "See it Now," "CBS Reports," "NBC White Paper," "NET Journal," and ABC's four-hour special on Africa. Onwards and upwards.

But there is another great tradition in documentary films, a different tradition. The fact that it is so neglected in television is strange—since its first great exponent, its first supreme originator, was an American. I mean, of course, Robert Flaherty, and I mean his unforgettable characters of "Nanook of the North," "Man of Aran," and "Louisiana Story." I mean the tradition of human revelations, the personal documentary. In Flaherty's work we see the distinguishing characteristics of this kind of documentary—not great issues, but human events in human scale, a man trying to catch a seal through the ice; not topicality but timelessness, the eternal struggle of man against nature; not fact and information but emotion, drama, a boy shrinking in fright at his first view of an oil derrick; not expertise and authority but ordinary human beings swept up in the current of life; not objectivity but a sense of the guts of people, a deep involvement; not a forum for the presentation of ideas but life itself; not journalism but art; not education but drama; not words but pictures; not logic but sentiment; not rationality but tears, rage and tenderness; not the reporter but a poet.

In all personal documentaries—Flaherty's and those of his successors today, Pennebaker, Leacock and Bill Jersey—a similar pattern is followed: a person whom we get to know and care about is confronted with a problem. It is a problem we can all identify with personally. He surmounts this problem, or fails to surmount it, but we live through it with him. The problem is not irrelevant to the great issues of our time. In the great personal documentaries the issues are there, but they are not the starting point; the human being is the starting point. The social issue is the backdrop against which the human drama unfolds itself.

Jersey's "A Time for Burning" is an example. Race relations provide a backdrop for the film, but we are really involved with the minister of a Lutheran church in Omaha. He wants to take a very small step forward. He wants his parishioners, on a voluntary basis, to exchange home visits with the members of Omaha's black Lutheran church. The Reverend is caught between the militant Black Nationalists, who scorn this step as too tentative—"Your Christ is a phony," they say—and the elders of his own church, who see this step as too revolutionary. The Reverend is ground down under the pressures and is forced to resign from his church. But the film grips like a good novel; the plot sweeps us along, man's humanity and inhumanity are revealed.

"A Time for Burning" was offered to CBS but was turned down, and in a list of last season's films you will not find anything like it. Where on that list is a film about a young man who flees to Canada to repudiate the draft? Where on that list is a film about a man whose marriage is breaking up; or a film about a middle-aged man, mortgaged to the hilt and laid off from his job at an ad agency; or the film about the lonely girl searching for a man through an endless procession of "singles" weekends at Grossinger's? Where is the story of the teeny-bopper who leaves home for Haight-Ashbury; or the story of the man suffering his first coronary; or the story of the factory worker, scraping the money together to marry his daughter and satisfy his wife's social-climbing ambitions? These films are not on the list, not on the air, and not even in the planning stage. They have taken the life out of the film. Why they have done it is something to wonder about.

Part of the problem is that the people in charge—presidents and vice-presidents in charge of news for the network—come out of the tradition of reportage. Many of them worked for news-papers or magazines before television, or for radio. They are word people. They worked through World War II, many of them, on films like "Why We Fight," or "The M-1 Rifle," or "Your Office of Price Administration," or "How to Dig A Sanitary Ditch." They are newsmen. They pride themselves on being reporters.

These network newsmen are not hip to the new film—that is important to realize. The kind of equipment that makes it really possible to get inside your subjects, to follow them quietly with a minimum of interference and direction, to reveal their essence, is something relatively new. Fast film, the shoulder brace and the hand-held camera, the quiet 16mm Eclair, the Nagra, the radio mike, the camera and sound operating independently, without a cord to connect them but still in synch—all this, and especially the filmmakers' sensibilities that accompany the equipment, is fairly new. Call it Cinema Verite, Direct Cinema, the Underground Film or what you will. The network establishment has not caught up with it yet. They are still amortizing a lot of 35mm equipment and a lot of fairly ancient cameramen who are entrenched and impervious to change. The union hang-up is part of this. Try making a personal film with the grotesque kind of crew that the network-union contract sticks you with—cameramen, assistant cameramen, lighting men, sound men, assistant sound men, grips; sometimes ten or twelve men. "A Time For Burning" was made with two filmmakers.

The Federal Communications Commission, I suppose, is another reason why personal films are not made. There it is in black and white. To keep your license to broadcast, the FCC regulations say you must "inform the public on the vital issues of the day." Network politics is a factor, too. There is bad blood in every network between the programing department, the people who provide the entertainment, and the news department. There is competition for money and air time, and since they, the program people, make money, and we in news lose it, the programmers usually win the fight. That's why Fred Friendly quit CBS. He lost the fight. He wanted to put on George Kennan's testimony before the Senate Foreign Relations Committee; they wanted to put on a re-run of "I Love Lucy," and they did.

Not only does programing want us to be on the air as little as possible, but they also want us to stick to "our own thing." Our "own thing" is news, information. Vietnam? O.K. A film about a broken marriage? Why, that's not news, our soap operas take care of that. No.

So the news department must be careful about sticking to journalism.

But, beyond all this, there seems to me to be a deeper underlying reason why the personal documentary is notable chiefly for its absence. I think that reason is that we are living in an up-tight society. I think we are afraid of honest emotion. I think we dig all those facts and figures because they are so very remote. We can be detached. I think we are afraid in this America of tenderness; afraid of anger, afraid of laying our guts on the table. I think we feel that we have to keep the lid on very tight, because if we don't,

158

our kids are going to turn-on, the blacks are going to kill us, the poor are going to bust right into our living-rooms and slash up all that nice new furniture with machetes, our bank accounts are going down the drain, we are going to walk out on our marriages and our jobs and ball-it-up; the whole mess is going to come unglued. Fear exists, so we would rather keep it nice and cerebral. . . .

ARTHUR BARRON, producer-director of television documentaries, teacher, film-maker, quite in opposition to Theodore Koop argues for much more personal journalism in television—at least in the documentary. Barron contends that there are two traditions of the documentary film. One is the tradition of reportage—balanced, objective, fair presentation. It is this tradition which is overwhelmingly represented in the television documentary. The other tradition is the personal documentary which deals in human revelation. This tradition is virtually ignored in the television documentary. Yet without this element the film is lifeless, Barron says.

Barron has produced many important documentaries for television, both for the commercial networks and for public television. Among his productions are "Johnny Cash," "Sixteen in Webster Groves," and "The Great American Novel"—a trilogy. Barron has BA and MA degrees from Tulane University and a Ph.D. in sociology from Columbia University.

Since this article was written the situation in television has changed somewhat. CBS no longer has a regularly scheduled documentary hour every Tuesday evening. This has been replaced by occasional documentary hours plus "60 Minutes," a weekly television "magazine" usually made up of several featurettes. Television may have begun to move tentatively toward more personal documentaries. Occasionally on "60 Minutes" one sees glimpses of the kind of film Barron wishes television would produce. But these are still rare glimpses.

Is it legitimate to speak of a NEW JOURNALISM OF THE CINEMA? I think yes. There are at least two ways in which one may speak of New Journalism in the cinema.

The first view might be that taken by Vincent Canby in a New York Times review of the Costa-Gavras film, "State of Siege." Canby considers work such as Costa-Gavras' in "Siege" and also in "Z" and "Confession" to be a kind of New Journalism in that there merge in these films elements of journalism and elements of fiction. According to Canby the films have their roots in journalism, they look and sound like journalism, they adopt journalism's dispassionate tone, but "they are, first of all, fiction of an essential sort." This merger then becomes a New Journalism of the film much as a Wolfe or a Talese produces New Journalism in print by merging reporting with the techniques of fiction.

But there is a more elemental level on which one may speak of New Journalism in the cinema. We have contended in this book that at the core of the New Journalism is an increasing emphasis on individual liberty in the media. This tendency is to be found in the cinema also. In recent years there appears to have been some increase of individual liberty of expression in commercial filmmaking; however, it has not been great. The fullest liberty of individual expression in films is to be found in that portion of the cinema known variously as the underground cinema, experimental cinema or the New American Cinema. Here film artists have found they could create in almost total freedom. Artists such as Jack Smith and Andy Warhol sought and found a milieu in which they were free to do that which they would never be able to do in the commercial media.

Curiously, the underground cinema began to gain strength during the 1960's at about the same time that the New Journalism was stirring in the print media. Another interesting parallel is that just as New Journalists have affected mainstream journalism so have the underground filmmakers affected the commercial cinema—in both technique and subject matter.

160

17 | The Underground Film

By Charles C. Flippen

It goes by many names:
Avant-garde cinema
Experimental film
Film poetry
Independent film
New American cinema
Underground film

There is no universally accepted name for this movement—or more properly, film ethic, for that is what it really is. We will call it here the underground film. Though this term has unfortunate connotations (stealth, political machinations), it does at least tie the movement to other media activities of the past decade. And there are other connotations which quite accurately describe the underground film—low budget, make-do equipment, anti-establishment attitude.

The underground film appears in many forms—and frequently without apparent form. Its subject matter is virtually limitless.

The question might well be asked, with this great variety in name, subject matter and form how can one identify such an en-

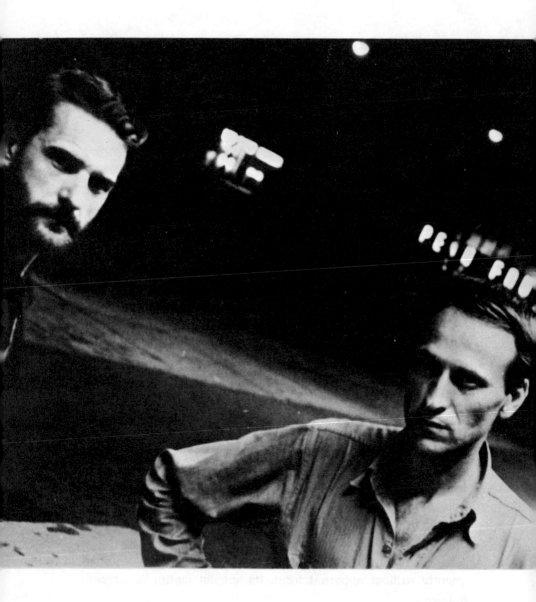

"*Guns of The Trees,*" by Jonas Mekas

tity as the underground film? Does the term really refer to anything? There is at least one element which gives unity to the films which go by these many names. That element is a personal artistic vision which these films express. The underground film differs from the Hollywood film which, even if it is very good, because of the corporate nature of its production can rarely express a personal artistic vision. It is this individual vision which dictates subject and imposes form on the underground film.

This quality of individual expression is perhaps the major feature of the underground film which ties it to the New Journalism of the last decade. The major thrust of the print media New Journalist has been toward greater freedom for personal expression—to write what he wants as he wants. It is the same purpose that leads the young filmmaker to the underground cinema. He realizes that there is no place in the film industry for him—or that he will have to compromise his vision to participate in the established industry. So just as his brother in the print media found he often had to go to the underground press to express himself, so the filmmaker joins the underground. And, as we shall see in detail later, just as the underground has had an effect on the establishment press, so too has the underground filmmaker had an impact upon the commercial cinema. There are other similarities of purpose, subject and form which will be considered later. First, let us look at the development of the underground film.

As with most movements, it is impossible to date precisely the beginning of the underground film. Some film historians date it from the early sixties. Others say it has been a part of the film since its inception. Most, however, see a development of the movement through certain periods culminating in the full-flowering of the sixties.* We will consider three periods of development here.

The first period occurred during the 1920's. This has frequently been called the period of the avant-garde film. It occurred following World War I and during a period of great political and social unrest. No doubt the atmosphere of the times plus

*See: Sheldon Renan, *An Introduction to the American Underground Film*, E. P. Dutton, New York, 1967.

the great experimentation in other art forms had much to do with this first wave of the art film.

The films produced during this period were often made by artists who worked principally in other media. They were heavily influenced by the Dada and Surrealist movements. Among the best known of those who produced films in those early years were Rene Clair, Man Ray, Luis Buñuel and Salvador Dali. Clair's most famous avant-garde effort is a dadaist piece called "Entr'acte" (1924). The film presents situations, events, objects which appear to bear little relation to one another. The most well-known scene is of a ballerina (with a beard) photographed by a camera beneath her feet. Undoubtedly the most famous of the early avant-garde films is "Un Chien Andalou" (1928) by Buñuel and Dali. This is the supreme surrealistic film. The opening scene indicates the nature of the film.

We see a man sharpening a razor. Then there is the head of a young woman. The blade is seen moving toward one of her eyes. The razor blade then slices into her eye.

The second period of development occurred during the forties. The non-commercial art films of this period were generally labelled experimental films. Among the names most closely associated with this period are Maya Deren, Sidney Peterson and Kenneth Anger. Deren's first film, and the one which in certain respects set the tone for the entire period, was "Meshes of the Afternoon" (1943). The film is quite surrealistic in nature. It concerns a young woman who is confronted in several situations by a knife. She finally kills herself with it. Deren was the first American to reach a wide audience with this kind of art film. Kenneth Anger, who of course continued to produce films, did his early work during the forties. His most well-known film from that period is "Fireworks" (1947), made when Anger was still a teenager. It is an explicitly homosexual film in which Anger, as the central character, dreams he is attacked by a group of sailors.

Jean Cocteau, an early maker of art films, is reported to have once said, "The cinema will only become an art when its raw materials are as cheap as pencil and paper." During the late fifties and more spectacularly in the sixties, something approximating

164

that must have happened. Suddenly there were more under-ground filmmakers (and this is when the term was applied to them) actively at work than even the aficionado could know and follow. Not only were there more people in the medium, but much more of quality was suddenly produced, also.

There were of course many causes of this sudden prolifera-tion. As the Cocteau statement suggests, equipment and material had become much more available—if still not cheap. But there was more than mere availability. Quite important was the fact that the earlier filmmakers, particularly those of the forties and fifties, became teachers in both a formal and informal sense. The atmosphere of the period also contributed. Any period of unrest seems to call forth an artistic response. And without doubt there occurred a major social revolution during this period. The spill-over affected all media. Finally, and perhaps of greatest signifi-cance, critical attention came to be focused on the field and some order began to develop in the distribution of the films. A central figure in both these endeavors has been Jonas Mekas. In fact many feel that without Mekas the underground film would not be as developed as it is today.

Probably the first organization to begin to bring order to the underground film industry was Cinema 16 which began as a club, but during the 1950's developed into a distribution agency for various kinds of films including the undergrounds. The Gryphon Group, an early attempt at collective film production, also dis-tributed films. Both organizations were eclipsed in the early six-ties by the Film-Makers' Cooperative, begun in 1962 by Jonas Mekas and others. A decision by Cinema 16 not to show a film by Stan Brakhage, "Anticipation of the Night," led to the creation of the Film-Makers' Cooperative by Mekas who believed in total freedom for the film maker and wanted to support that belief.

Mekas, who was born in Lithuania, came to this country in 1949 from a displaced persons camp in Germany. Three weeks after his arrival Mekas had a Bolex and was shooting film. In January, 1955 he brought out a periodical, *Film Culture*, which was to become the major critical organ for the underground film. Curiously, during those early years *Film Culture* was not entirely friendly to the undergrounds, calling them at one point "markedly adolescent." In 1958, Mekas began a column of film comment in the *Village Voice*. His work in both periodicals made Mekas the preeminent critical figure in the underground film during the 1960's and 1970's.

In the mid-sixties Mekas became convinced that the most pressing need of the underground was a place in which film-makers could show their films to the public. To this end he devoted great energies to establishing the Film-Makers Cinematheque. More recently he was instrumental in the establishment of the Anthology Film Archives, which opened in 1970. It shows, in repertory, the best of the underground films.

In addition to these many activities, Mekas has also been a filmmaker of importance himself. Many believe that his most recent films, such as "Diaries, Notes and Sketches" (1969) and "Reminiscences of a Journey to Lithuania" (1972), place him in the very forefront of artistic filmmakers. "Reminiscences" concerns a trip Mekas and his brother made to Lithuania in 1971. It is a nostalgic representation of what he saw and what it meant to him. "Diaries" deals, in a sense, with New York and people in the underground movement during the sixties. Both films are extraordinarily evocative and poetic in nature.

There are so many others active and important in the movement today that to attempt a listing here would be almost pointless. Two, however, must be mentioned. These are Andy Warhol and Stan Brakhage. Warhol is undoubtedly the most well-known of the American underground filmmakers. But to many Warhol is little more than a pop artist showman who mocks the film art with anti-film pictures such as "Empire" (1964), an eight hour study of the Empire State Building, and "Eat" (1963)—a film of a man eating. Most, however, accepted him as an important artist with the appearance of "The Chelsea Girls" in 1966. The film consists of twelve incidents supposedly taking place in the Chelsea Hotel. The scenes concern, among other things, homosexuality, lesbianism and drug-taking. It became the underground's first popular success.

Brakhage is considered by Mekas to be the most important

168

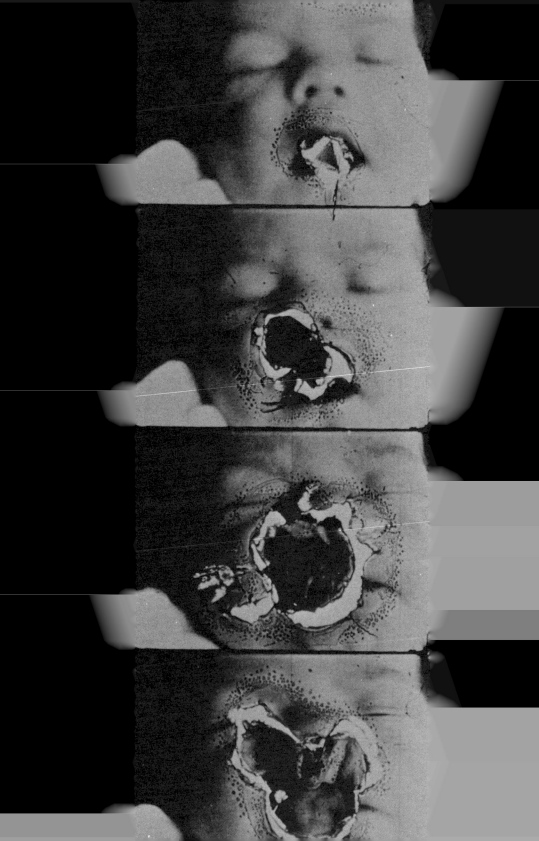

filmmaker in America today. His most influential works are "Dog Star Man/Art of Vision" (1965) and "Songs" (1964-). "Dog Star Man" centers around a woodsman and his dog. The camera photographs what the man sees, photographs the man, photographs his internal organs. In intricacy the film has been compared to James Joyce's *Finnegans Wake*. "Songs" are mostly brief works dealing with elements of daily life.

The impetus, growth, direction and impact of the underground cinema during the sixties and seventies has paralleled that of the underground print media. Just as elements of the underground film existed very early in the history of the film, so too were there very early papers akin to the underground press. But the full flowering of both did not occur until the sixties. The impetus for this growth in both media was quite similar. Important factors already alluded to were the social atmosphere of the times and the rigidity of the established media.

In recent years, both underground media have had a very direct influence on their establishment sires. Some of this has come by imitation. The establishment has seen the undergrounds succeed—indeed garner acclamation. And so they have adopted some of their techniques. Additionally, a number of those people who served their apprenticeships with the underground media have now gone into the established media and there are personally applying what they learned in these apprenticeships. In the commercial film we see the effects of this in such things as the bolder treatment of once taboo subject matter and in the more creative use of the camera—for example, the now common use of the hand-held camera. Indeed, there is at present a more general willingness to experiment.

Where the future will take the underground media in general and the underground film in particular is of course unanswerable in absolute terms. Most likely there will be a tapering off of the hyperactivity of the sixties. We are already beginning to witness a renewed quiescence. Recent Supreme Court decisions (*i.e.*, Miller v. California, 1973) concerning pornography and obscenity may again make it difficult for some films to be seen—though one has hope that we are not going to go all the way back to the bad

171

old days. It is very likely that, just as with the underground newspaper, the best of underground filmmakers are going to become more and more establishment. To some extent we may be seeing this happen now as distribution becomes more orderly. We may also be seeing touches of this establishmentism in the underground films which tend increasingly to relate coherent narratives—and thereby to appeal presumably to larger audiences. But, also, there will always be the upstart. There will be someone with a new vision and the compulsion to bring that vision into being.

And that is vital. For it is always the new vision that prevents the old from dying—that rejuvenates it, that gives new life to the entire medium. It is the central thesis of this book that the New Journalism has helped free the old from its stultification. And this is certainly true of the film—particularly the American film. There are not many—save those who find value in camp or kitsch —who find artistic worth in most of what Hollywood produced in earlier decades. But in recent years there has been much produced by the commercial film industry which merits consideration. It didn't just happen. A dying industry learned from its bastard progeny. May the child continue to educate the parent.

18 | Public Access to the Media and Its Critics

By Jerome Barron

TWO TASKS WILL BE ATTEMPTED here. One is to appraise some of the more thoughtful criticism directed to the new movement for access to the media, both print and electronic. The other task is to reflect on one of the major constitutional or legal obstacles to the success of the movement for access to these media. This obstacle is what in legal terms is called the state action problem. The Constitution speaks of freedom of speech and press but the First Amendment has always been thought of, as has the Bill of Rights as a whole, as a limitation on government. The addresses of the constitutional command of freedom of speech and press are considered to be government officialdom. Indeed, until this century, so narrow was the scope of the Bill of Rights that it was thought to speak only to the federal government and not to the states. Gradually, the Supreme Court, particularly the Warren Court, through the process of interpreting the Fourteenth Amendment, brought the Bill of Rights to the state governments as well.

As a constitutional proposition, government repression of speech in the United States falls within the scope of the First

173

Amendment but private repression or avoidance of opinion does not. Is this a distinction which is still acceptable? We live in a day of single newspaper cities, of great newspaper chains, of vast networks which reach millions of people in an evening. In these forums political reputations develop and die. Entry to these forums is virtually the same as entry to public opinion itself.

Of course, there are those who believe that this identity of the mass media with the opinion process is over-stated.

The conventional rationale of broadcast regulation is that the broadcast media are limited access media. Since broadcasting by its technology is not open to all, the broadcaster must be required by law to serve as a trustee for the entire community in all its variety and its contrariety of viewpoint. On the same basis, the communities served by the print media, particularly the readership of daily newspapers, should have some rights of entry into the papers that serve their communities. Most cities of any size have some VHF television stations, but only half a hundred cities in the nation have competitive daily newspaper situations.

The Constitution, of course, has been interpreted to apply only to state action. Private power, no matter what its magnitude, is considered to be beyond the reach of the Constitution generally and the First Amendment in particular. From the classic view of the American law of freedom of expression, this is no particular problem since that law presumes the existence of a self-operating marketplace of ideas which marches sublimely on unless government interferes. But a free marketplace of ideas does not exist. Media power, when it is power of great magnitude and impact, should be suffused with a modicum of responsibility and accountability. Clearly this position runs against the grain of the classic laissez-faire approach to freedom of the press in this country.

In the electronic media, the movement for access to the media was granted a First Amendment basis in the Supreme Court's celebrated *Red Lion*[1] case where it was held that not only was the fairness doctrine consistent with the First Amendment but that fairness and access were First Amendment necessities. Imposition of legal responsibilities in broadcasting has not posed the same obstacle that affirmative First Amendment responsibili-

174

ties for the print media have presented to the courts.

In fact, the access front is still being projected forward in the broadcast media. In a recent case, *Business Executives' Move for Vietnam Peace v. FCC,*[2] a panel of the United States Court of Appeals for the District of Columbia, by divided vote, held that access for spot announcements for political and social ideas, could not, as a general proposition, be banished from the airwaves. To do so would inhibit political ideas at the expense of the commercial; for commercial advertising, the warp and woof of the financial base of television, need not fear such banishment. In a seminal opinion, which is now under review by the Supreme Court of the United States, Judge Wright held that to prefer the commercial over the political would be to invert the traditional conception of the purpose of free speech.

But this holding requires a preliminary step. It requires inquiry into one of the basic questions of contemporary American life: may power exercised by private individuals or particularly private broadcast corporations be constitutionalized? The Court of Appeals was convinced that constitutional obligation should not be avoided in broadcasting because censorship is being wielded by private broadcasters rather than government officials.

Judge Wright said that individual broadcasters would be submitted to constitutional obligation because they were licensed to use the airwaves. They have a three-year permit to use the frequencies and nothing more. In this sense, all their power is derivative from government.

In a recent article critical of the movement for access to the media, Professor Louis Jaffe, a distinguished scholar in public law, belittles the significance of the licensing idea as a basis for imposing constitutional obligation on the electronic media. He denies that the commodity which is licensed, the airwaves, really belongs to the public or for that matter, the government. Jaffe writes:[3]

> The popular cliche, that the broadcaster is using the 'public's airwaves' is a vague and intermediate concept. I think we would have heard little of it had not the existing

175

technology required regulation of broadcasting to avoid interference. For in one way or another, we all use air and space. To speak of owning such resources is a solecism.

This viewpoint is only possible if one assumes that the present system of broadcasting is inevitable and immutable. It is interesting that the Supreme Court does not find the present structure of the broadcasting pre-ordained. In its unanimous opinion for the Supreme Court in the *Red Lion* case, Mr. Justice White pointed out that licensees had no proprietary rights in their licenses.[4] Moreover, he pointed out that as a legal matter there was absolutely no reason, except perhaps that of practicality, why the broadcast day could not be parcelled out among each of 200,000,000 Americans.

In my view, those who are licensed by the government, under the circumstances broadcasters are so licensed, may not do what the government itself cannot do, *i.e.*, censor political ideas to the advantage of commercialism. Government would be prohibited by the First Amendment from embarking on a policy of censorship and therefore those temporarily licensed by the government are so limited by the First Amendment as well.

Professor Jaffe's rejoinder to this argument, the position that broadcasting is state action because it is regulated, is as follows:[5]

We are each of us private centers of power and initiative, and it would be ironic to conclude that if in the public interest a person or an enterprise must be very much regulated, his actions by reason of that very liability become the actions of the state.

What is objectionable in this approach is that it refuses to make any distinctions of scale among private power aggregates. Obviously, each person is, or ought to be, (depending on how seriously one takes the Puritan ethic) a private center of initiative. But compared to the individual, CBS, NBC, or the Hearst newspaper chain, or the Scripps-Howard chain is quite a different center of power and initiative.

Professor Jaffe apparently finds it "maddening" that

176

"hysterical overestimation of media power"[6] should lead to changes in constitutional doctrine. Such criticism is an excellent illustration of what Marshall McLuhan calls the failure of print-oriented man to come to terms with the new electronic media.

The distinguished First Amendment scholar, Professor Thomas I. Emerson, is a good deal more sympathetic to access than Professor Jaffe. Professor Emerson has said that "a limited right of access to the press can be safely enforced."[7] Yet he writes that the presence of scarcity in the daily newspaper field, in terms of this "untapped demand for diversity," should not be assessed by counting the number of daily newspapers but rather by looking "to the number of printing presses."[8]

However, the number of printing presses does not seem relevant to either a scarcity inquiry or a power inquiry. The so-called prestige media, the city daily newspaper, the VHF commercial television network affiliate, are the prime vehicles of opinion. It is the control of these media that gives the owners and operators of the media their enormous power over ideas. That a few heretics here and there may garner a printing press is simply no match or counterpoise for such power, particularly when one recalls that in recent years some members of the printers' unions have exhibited a particular distaste for heresy.

Professor Jaffe's rejoinder to the argument that the very power of the media demands constitutionalization is that all private activity is in a sense an exercise of power. But this position is waning in force in American constitutional law. Gradually, many modes of private power are being constitutionalized. The law is learning to make distinctions within the private sector rather than merely holding that anything that is privately-owned is therefore a constitutional no-man's land. Recent developments on the interpretation of state action in constitutional law are illustrative. Besides the fact that the imposition of a structure of First Amendment duties on private broadcasters would seem to have settled the state action problem for broadcasting, recent case law certainly indicates that the pervasiveness of government regulation can render otherwise private activity sufficiently quasi-public to submit the activity to constitutional standards of duty.

In a recent and not unrepresentative federal case in New York, two women, members of the National Organization of Women (NOW), sought to end the practice of McSorley's Old Ale House in New York City of refusing to serve women at its bar on the ground that the practice constituted a denial of rights received by the Equal Protection Clause of the Fourteenth Amendment. But McSorley's was a privately-owned bar just as a newspaper is privately owned. Constitutional obligation, the argument ran, could not be imposed on a bar any more than it could be imposed on a newspaper.

But bars like broadcasters operate on licenses conferred by government. Judge Mansfield holding for the women's organization said as follows:[9]

> The reasoning in favor of finding state action is that the state license enables the private licensee to engage in discriminatory conduct in the exercise of its franchise rights. To put it another way, without the state license to serve beer, defendant here could never have discriminated in the sale of beer. The license, it is argued, becomes a license to discriminate.
>
> *   *   *
>
> We believe that the present case is distinguishable from those licensing cases where courts have shied away from finding state action, because here we are not dealing merely with a bare state licensor-licensee relationship. In addition we are faced with a pervasive regulation by the state of the activities of the defendant, a commercial enterprise engaged in voluntarily serving the public except for women.

Refusal to tolerate the denial of freedom of expression to a licensee in an industry characterized by pervasive regulation is thus by no means an unusual basis for submitting private actor to constitutional responsibilities. The pervasiveness of regulation, the dependence on licensing is if anything more acute, because of

178

the stakes involved, in broadcasting than it is by the activity regulated in *McSorley's* case.

A critic might say at this point: perhaps, given the current
state of the law, you have furnished a basis for state action in the
electronic media, but how do you show such a basis with regard
to the print media? Are you suggesting that the press be licensed?
The answer is no. But one might look at the print media's dependence on the second class mailing rate, and then reflect on the
present ruckus against the proposed increase in that rate. The
print media do not find the First Amendment offended if government gives them a subsidy. They should also not find the First
Amendment offended if the state involvement represented by the
subsidy authorizes at least a limited right of access as a matter of
constitutional compulsion. Surely, such a conclusion strains
neither logic nor justice.

Professor Jaffe gives short shrift to the view that when great
powers of censorship are placed in the hands of a few who control the throttles of opinion that power should be constitutionalized even though it is nominally private. Says Professor Jaffe:[10]

The proposition that the threat of government is much
less than that of private censorship cannot withstand the
lesson of the government's attempt to suppress
publication of the Pentagon Papers.

First of all, Professor Jaffe has shifted the ground of debate.
None of the people he identifies with this position, Commissioner
Nicholas Johnson, Professor Jerrold Walden or myself, have contended that private censorship is worse than public censorship.
What has been said is that there is little to choose between them.
Fred Friendly put it well at Congressional hearings in the fall of
1971, when he said that then-Vice President Agnew and the networks deserve each other. It is power that must be
constitutionalized whether public or private.

As for the *Pentagon Papers* case itself, that episode hardly
illustrates the power of government and the weakness of media
power.

What actually happened in the case? *The New York Times*
published the Papers and the *Washington Post* followed suit. The

179

Boston Globe, the *St. Louis Post-Dispatch,* the *St. Louis Globe-Democrat,* to name just a few, stood in line to publish the *verboten* material. In a virtual frenzy to publish that which any student of Southeast Asian studies had known for years, the American press found themselves in an ideal position. They stood ready to publish in all its muddy density whatever secrets could be deduced from the Pentagonese in which the Pentagon Papers were written. Better yet, the Justice Department was obtuse enough to prosecute the press for publishing. A safe issue and a natural enemy—the perfect combination for the journalism of the dominant media establishment. It was a dream come true, a battle that could not be lost. The Supreme Court was hurried into rendering a quick decision. Nine separate opinions were delivered.[11] More time might have produced a single opinion. The opinions of the Justices were less enchanted by this demonstration of press virility than the excited journalists who bored the nation with their heroism for weeks. It is only those who have lived in countries where media power is nil and government power is everything that know how impossible heralding such a conflict would be in a totalitarian country.

Some of the Justices mentioned that the publishers, Arthur Ochs Sulzburger and Katharine Graham, might have violated federal legislation in receiving and publishing the information and these Justices hinted indictments against the publishers might be upheld consistently with the First Amendment. But no indictments ever have been forthcoming. The person chosen for prosecution was not a mighty publisher but the true man of courage in the case, the man who provided the material, Daniel Ellsberg.

There is a difficulty in the sense by which media realities are perceived by even sympathetic scholars in the First Amendment area. Some remarks of Professor Emerson are instructive on this point:[12]

> The distinction the Federal Communications Commission makes between a requirement that the licensee broadcast programs within its general categories, and control over the contents of a particular program,

conforms exactly to the theory that the government can take measures to expand the variety of expression but may not censor the actual expression itself.

This states current First Amendment law. However, the ideal of expansion of the variety of expression is somewhat thwarted because no distinction is made between various power strengths within the broadcast industry. The problem of the independent producer versus the network and the problem of the independent licensee competing with the network-affiliate licensee are all avoided by pretending that the licensee is the single and important power unit in broadcasting. Protecting the licensee's freedom to make individual programing decisions is basically a farce. The enormous power of the network to determine what programing will occupy prime time renders the various affiliates mere conduits for the network. These realities are all ignored under the approach that freedom for the broadcast licensee secures freedom of expression in television. The greater the concentration of power the greater the obligation for public access. The individual station licensee is currently the fellow who must scrap with the local citizens' group. But the real target for the citizens' group and for the access movement should be the network.

We must become a great deal more sophisticated about censorship than we have been. The private censor in the form of network officials making programing decisions which affect millions and the local disc jockey deciding which record to play may both be viewed alike as performing an editorial function. Similarly, both can be viewed as performing a censorship function, or less pejoratively, a gatekeeper function. But surely the power differential between the network executive and the disc jockey should not be completely disregarded. The purpose of a constitutional order is to submit power to procedures which make it responsive to the will of the larger polity. The greater that power, the larger influence or spell it is in a position to cast over the polity as a whole, the greater the case for subjecting it to criticism and responsibility. I do not find this concept to be unreal nor do I believe it is in any sense foreign to our constitutionalism.

In analyzing my suggestion that "the newspaper must be viewed as impressed with a public service stamp and hence under an obligation to provide space on a non-discriminatory basis to representative groups in the community,"[13] Professor Emerson says that four modes of access for the print media can be envisioned. The first category would be a duty to publish paid non-commercial editorial advertisements. The second category would establish a right of reply by providing equal space for those libelled or personally attacked. The third category would be to require papers to open their "letters to the editor" column or some other area for "statements by individuals or groups or issues not reported or on viewpoints not represented by the paper." The fourth and last mode of access would be to require the press to provide for coverage of all newsworthy "subject matter and expression of all responsible viewpoints."

Professor Emerson believes that the realization of the first two kinds of access would be consistent with the First Amendment but that the implementation of the third and fourth would not.

A right to the non-discriminatory publication of editorial advertisements and a right of reply for personal and libellous attacks have always been the focal point of my concern for access to the print media. In this respect a more limited right of access is being advocated for the press than now obtains in broadcasting.

Whether a huge administrative apparatus would be necessary to enforce an access approach to the print media involving the third and fourth categories thus engendering government surveillance threatening press freedom is a good question. But it is a premature question.

Professor Emerson has addressed himself to the frontier issue in the question of access to the print media. How do we secure true access as distinguished from a right of reply in the print media? Few would wish to accomplish access to the print media by creating a new bureaucracy. Certainly no federal agency or authority should oversee the press.

But we have more immediate problems to solve. A growing

core of agreement, even within the press, for one mode of access, the duty to publish editorial advertisements, is still far short of realization. True suppression of a point of view which seeks but is denied an award of space in a given community daily is more likely to come about when no opportunity to buy an ad exists. But a right to publish editorial advertisements is still not established. The courts consistently reject it. State action is the problem—at least it is the problem which saps solution at the level of judicial creativity.

Some of our contemporary problems in freedom of expression would benefit from some application of the law that has been applied to another First Amendment area, the area of freedom of religion. Where free exercise is impossible without some government aid, affirmative legislation is considered legitimate. Thus, provision for voluntary worship in the armed forces is considered to be constitutionally valid. As Professor Wilbur Katz has written:[14]

Affirmative government action to maintain religious freedom in these instances serves the secular purpose of promoting a constitutional right, the free exercise of religion.

Of course the analogy is not a tight fit. In the religious situations, government is taking the affirmative action itself without requiring any new duties of private actors as rights of access to the media necessarily involve. Nevertheless, the constitutional problem, the textual problem, is if anything greater in terms of permitting affirmative government action in aid of religion because one of the components of the American definition of freedom of religion is a prohibition against establishment. Government aid to freedom of expression is not prohibited as a textual matter nor should it be as a practical matter. Without such aid through legislation or through judicial interpretation, freedom of expression would be no more a reality than free exercise of religion would be in the military.

The outermost extremity of the access problem is the issue of when a particular view (or views) is being under-represented in a community's media outlets. It is an intriguing problem because in cities across the land with one daily newspaper or one VHF television outlet a section of the populace, be it a Chicano group or a black group or a union, has the feeling that they have no entry, no voice in the dominant opinion forum of the community in which they live. But estimating how to determine when a group should be represented and when an opinion has been suppressed or under-represented is obviously a task of enormous ambiguity and difficulty. Institutionally, what persons or agency should undertake such a task is no less baffling.

It is appropriate to talk about this problem. But the practical and constitutional difficulties it raises should not deflect energy from doing what can be done.

Let me give you an illustration of the kind of problem which concerns me and the kind of problem I think we can solve. The Green Bay Press-Gazette is the only daily newspaper serving Brown County, Wisconsin, which has a population of 160,000. A local group in Green Bay, Problem Pregnancy Counselors, which among other tasks makes abortion referrals, wants to place an ad in the Green Bay Press-Gazette which states as follows:

"Problem Pregnancy Counseling Service. For Referral call 437-9008."

The Press-Gazette had earlier run this ad as a public service until the Press-Gazette advised Problem Pregnancies that the ad would no longer be run because Problem Pregnancies counseled abortion.

Problem Pregnancies' efforts to place the ad through the Press-Gazette's classified advertising failed. Problem Pregnancies were given two reasons for failure to run the ad. First, they were told that Section 143-075 of the Wisconsin statutes prohibits, among other things, any newspaper from publishing the advertisement of abortion. From an access point of view, the presence of the statute is quite interesting and shows the woodenness and the perversity of the state action problem. The state is the censor here, and the newspaper the enforcer of state censorship. Therefore, arguably, if the censorship involved violates the First Amendment, then the necessary state action exists to impose by case law an affirmative duty on the part of the press not

184

to follow the state law command of censorship but rather to heed an implicit constitutional command providing for freedom of expression.

The second reason given Problem Pregnancies by the *Press-Gazette* for refusing to publish the ads is that the *Press-Gazette* disapproves of the policies or actions of Problem Pregnancies. Presently, the *Press-Gazette* requires all who advertise in its "personal" column to sign statements of their purpose and activities. Such an inquiry, with its obvious impingement on freedom of association and freedom of expression, is an intriguing illustration of the power that is available to the print media to be as repressive and as exclusive in guarding the entrances to the market place of ideas as any bigoted government.

Remember that the *Green Bay Press-Gazette* had never in print counseled abortion. Mr. Stephen Cohen of the Northeastern Wisconsin Chapter of the American Civil Liberties Union believed that the case was distinguishable from a celebrated access case decided in 1971 whereby the refusal of all four Chicago newspapers to publish a union ad criticizing the sale by Marshall Field of foreign-made textiles was held to be permissible. Cohen believes that the *Chicago Joint Board* case[15] and this case differ in that Green Bay is a monopoly newspaper market whereas in Chicago there were four dailies. This certainly is a distinction that the court in *Chicago Joint Board* encouraged. But it is an approach more suitable in antitrust cases which deal with lack of competition in a particular commodity or industry. From a First Amendment point of view, the question should be whether complete censorship as a fact exists in a community's daily newspaper market. Whether one daily newspaper or four are published is hardly significant if all four papers are so cowed by a particular advertiser that no space will be sold to any group criticizing those advertisers on political or social grounds.

Whether the fact of state compulsion in a situation like the one in Green Bay would embolden a federal district court to require access for a viewpoint which the state has not set itself against is an interesting question. But it is deeply disturbing that such matters should turn on such technical distinctions. The

185

same Seventh Circuit which declined to say that a union had a right to buy space in any daily newspaper nevertheless managed to hold that a state university student newspaper which refused to accept certain anti-Vietnam war ads violated the First Amendment.[16] Why? Because in the university situation, the key point for the Court was that it was a state university and therefore the necessary state action was present.

Whether access to the campus press is less important than access to the general press is an interesting question. Whatever the answer to it, the fact of the matter is that since so much of higher education is under state sponsorship, the one area where the law has really developed a right of access is that of the state university campus press.

Another ground of difference with the *Chicago Joint Board* case, according to Mr. Cohen, was that the ad was ostensibly rejected in Chicago because of its content while here the ad was rejected because of the paper's hostility to the ideas of its sponsors.

This is a distinction worth pursuing. Oversight over content is, after all, an editorial matter. But oversight over ideas, hostility to an ideology no matter how expressed or how practiced, is the enemy of freedom of information, of diversity of opinion, of all the things that the First Amendment is thought to stand for.

If the responsibilities of implementing First Amendment values required a monopoly paper to publish all paid political and social advertisements, then the paper should not be held liable if someone in the community considered that such an ad libelled him. The libel plaintiff in that event should be directed for compensation to the group or individual which purchased the ad. In the now famous *New York Times v. Sullivan* case,[17] the Court spoke to the great social value inherent in the editorial advertisement in terms of the function of providing access for the community. But the Court assured that it was entirely appropriate that the paper, rather than the civil rights groups which sponsored the ad, should be a libel plaintiff. As a consequence, the Court has been forced to largely reduce the opportunity to legally protect the values of privacy and reputation in our society. The pressure which has fed this pervasive attack on privacy and reputa-

186

tion would have been greatly reduced if the Court had held in *New York Times* what it had earlier held for broadcasting: where a duty existed to provide equal time, apart from the wishes of a broadcaster, the broadcaster then should be immunized from liability.[18]

In the Green Bay, Wisconsin access case, the Legal Director of the American Civil Liberties Union, Melvin Wulf, said that organization must, if only for symbolic purposes, take the view that newspapers are sacrosanct from government regulation which would have any effect at all upon their content. Mr. Wulf wrote the Wisconsin local as follows:

"When there was some question whether the Illinois division of the ACLU would file an amicus brief in support of the petition for certiorari in the *Chicago Joint Board* case, I told David Goldberger that if they did, he should look forward to an amicus curiae brief on the other side by the National office. Likewise Wisconsin. That's not a threat, it's a promise."

Mr. Wulf sent me a copy of his manifesto.

It is difficult not to admire the fervor of this defense of the press. But it is a fervor that is misplaced. It confuses the property rights of the publisher with the primary value behind freedom of the press which is full, fair and free discussion of ideas.

This impassioned refusal to impose responsibilities on the press is an example of the romantic view of the First Amendment. The idea is that if government is excluded from any connection with the press, the free market mechanism of ideas will necessarily assure the required information, participation and debate indispensible to democratic self-government. But this portrait, and therefore its defense, is neither real nor true. Non-governmental power combinations have contorted the marketplace theory truth beyond recognition. It is the newspaper chains and the broadcast networks that now dispense and collect the tickets for admission to the "marketplace of ideas."

Professor Jaffe argues that even if the dominant print and television media are closed, there are other "avenues of expression."[19] From a First Amendment point of view, this is not a very persuasive argument. What we are interested in is the protection of the integrity of the primary forums of public opinion because these are the forums where the battle for public opinion is shaped, fought and won. Richard Jencks of CBS once said to me: "What you people want is our audience for your ideas." Precisely.

But the reasons for this should be understood. The advantage the prestige media, and the concomitant constitutional obligation they should be under as a result, was underscored by the Supreme Court in *Red Lion*. The Court conceded that although media alternatives may be available, nevertheless it was access to the prestige media that was crucial. Mr. Justice White summarized for the Court the importance of the prestige media:[20]

> Even where there are gaps in spectrum utilization, the fact remains that existing broadcasters have often attained their present position because of their initial government selection in competition with others before new technological advances opened new opportunities for further uses. Long experience in broadcasting, confirmed habits of listeners and viewers, network affiliation, and other advantages in program procurement give existing broadcasters a substantial advantage over new entrants even where new entry is technologically possible. These advantages are the fruit of a preferred position conferred by the Government. Some present possibility for new entry by competing stations is not enough, in itself, to render unconstitutional the Government's effort to assure that a broadcaster's programming ranges widely enough to serve the public interest.

In summary, we find our theory of freedom of the press undergoing severe re-examination. This examination is long overdue. In the law of libel, the Supreme Court has made some radical revisions: it is more difficult to secure a libel judgment today against either the print or the broadcast media than it has ever been. These new immunities have all been established to secure a constitutional value, vigorous, robust debate of public issues. But looking at the media today we cannot turn away from the fact that its pattern of control and ownership is monopolisitc. Monopolists are not very good debaters. The press should forgive its critics if some of them fear that monopolists may sometimes forget to debate.

There are now signs that the Supreme Court has begun to realize that freedom of the press is not entirely a matter of immunity from law but it may sometimes entail responsibility under law. In *Rosenbloom v. Metromedia,* the Court extended the relative immunity the media enjoyed from libel litigation to any case where a public issue has been discussed. The plurality opinion for the Court for the first time recognized that access to the media might be a constitutional necessity. Mr. Justice Brennan, speaking for the Court, said in an opinion joined by Chief Justice Burger and Mr. Justice Blackmun:[21]

> If the States fear that private citizens will not be able to respond adequately to publicity involving them, the solution lies in the direction of ensuring their ability to respond, rather than in a stifling public discussion of matters of public concern.

The Court said further:[22]

> It is important to recognize that the private individual often desires press exposure either for himself, his ideas, or his causes. Constitutional adjudication must take into account the individual's interest in access to the press as well as the individual's interest in preserving his reputation.

These remarks raise intriguing possibilities for the future. If constitutional adjudication can recognize a right of individual access to the press, does this mean that the state action problem is in fact surmountable? Can a right of access be fashioned by the courts? After all, the court speaks of adjudication rather than legislation. The immediate future may well provide some answers to these questions. Critics of the movement for access to the media have quite properly raised the many problems, legal and practical, that surround recognition of a right of access. But despite these difficulties future constitutional adjudication will increasingly recognize a right of access to the media, both print and electronic.

EDITOR'S NOTE: Since this article was written, there have been two important developments in the field. The *BEM* case discussed in the text was reversed by the Supreme Court. *Columbia Broadcasting System, Inc. v. Democratic National Committee*, 93 S. Ct. 2080 (1973). At the same time, the Florida Supreme Court has upheld a Florida law requiring a right of reply to the press for a political candidate during a campaign. *Tornillo v. Miami Herald*, S. Ct. of Florida, Case No. 43,009, Per Curiam, *Slip* Opinion, July 18, 1973. The case is now being reviewed by the Supreme Court.

[1] *Red Lion Broadcasting Co. v. FCC*, 395 U.S. 367 (1969).
[2] 450 F. 2d 642 (D.C. Cir. 1971).
[3] Jaffe, "The Editorial Responsibility of the Broadcaster: Reflections on Fairness and Access," 85 Harvard L. Rev. 768 at 783 (1972).
[4] *Red Lion Broadcasting Co. v. FCC*, 395 U.S. 367 (1969).
[5] Jaffe, "The Editorial Responsibility of the Broadcaster: Reflections on Fairness and Access," 85 Harv. L. Rev. 768 at 783 (1972).
[6] *Ibid.*
[7] Emerson, *The System of Free Expression*, 671 (1970).
[8] *Id.* at 662.
[9] *Seidenberg v. McSorley's Old Ale House, Inc.*, 317 F. Supp. 593 at 598-599 (S.D.N.Y. 1970).
[10] Jaffe, "The Editorial Responsibility of the Broadcaster: Reflections on Fairness and Access," 85 Harv. L. Rev. 768 at 786 (1972).
[11] *New York Times v. United States*, 403 U.S. 713 (1971).
[12] Emerson, *The System of Free Expression*, 666 (1970).
[13] Emerson, *The System of Free Expression*, 670 (1970).
[14] See Katz, *Note on the Constitutionality of Shared Time*, 1964 Relig. & Pub. Order 85, 88.
[15] *Chicago Joint Board, Amalgamated Clothing Workers of America, AFL-CIO v. Chicago Tribune Company*, 435 F. 2d 470 (7th Cir. 1970); cert. den. 91 S. Ct. 1662 (1971).
[16] *Lee v. Board of Regents*, 441 F. 2d 1257 (7th Cir. 1971).
[17] 376 U.S. 245 (1964).
[18] *Farmers Educational and Cooperative Union of America v. WDAY*, 360 U.S. 525 (1959).
[19] Jaffe, "The Editorial Responsibility of the Broadcaster: Reflections on Fairness and Access," 85 Harv. L. Rev. 768 at 789 (1972).
[20] *Red Lion Broadcasting Co. v. FCC*, 395 U.S. 367 at 400 (1969).
[21] *Rosenbloom v. Metromedia*, 403 U.S. 29 at 47 (1971).
[22] *Id.* at 47, footnote 15.

JEROME BARRON, *Professor of Law at the National Law Center of George Washington University, broaches in his article an area much different from that discussed elsewhere in this book—public access to the media. The concept of public access suggests that the public has a right of access to the media—that is, the right to have its message carried by the media. This subject area differs from the others considered here in that it is an external pressure applied to liberalize the media. All of the other elements of this movement toward liberation have been from within—from people already associated with the media who are insisting upon greater freedom in the performance of their roles. But public access may be considered part of the New Journalism in that it, too, is forcing the media to consider more closely the individual.*

In his article Barron argues strongly for a legal right of access. He argues that there is both a need for public access and legal justification for such a right. He feels that there is a First Amendment right involved—that the public has rights in the media just as do media proprietors.

Barron is the former dean of the Syracuse University College of Law. He has also taught at the Universities of North Dakota, New Mexico and Saskatchewan. He is the author of Freedom of the Press for Whom? *and co-author of* Mass Communication Law: Cases and Comment.

19 Considerations on the Future of American Journalism

By Ben H. Bagdikian

JOURNALISTS TODAY are asking themselves more and more about their future. And it is not surprising that they are asking. For one thing, today governmental attacks on printed and broadcast journalism are exceptionally virulent, more in what is called peacetime than at any period in American history except during the time of the Alien and Sedition Acts.

These official attacks are not just complaints and denunciations. A free press should expect that. After all, the press has a license to criticize everything in sight and there is no reason it should be immune from the same treatment.

What is alarming today are official attacks not just on the press but legal attacks by government on the constitutional basis for a free press. The government has seriously attempted and partially succeeded, for the first time in United States history, in obtaining court-ordered prior censorship.[1] It is now engaged in

[1] In the summer of 1971, the Nixon administration attempted to halt newspaper publication of the so-called Pentagon Papers—a classified government study of U.S. involvement in Vietnam through 1968. By court injunction they succeeded in stopping publication for up to fifteen days. A Supreme Court decision freed the newspapers to resume publication.

threats of criminal prosecution of journalists and their organizations who choose not to become instruments of official policy.[2]

Such behavior in totalitarian countries or in those nations with no tradition of a free press is familiar. But this is something new and ominous in the United States.

The future of journalism is also a natural question in the face of uncertainty about the adequacy of all institutions. The United States is in a period of profound self-examination when citizens are asking how much the traditional social organization fits a changed environment. The validity of the standard press quite appropriately comes under that same kind of examination, that is, whether its usual practices and performance are appropriate for the 1970's and 1980's.

The radical left has about decided that the standard press is an instrument of the status quo and an enemy of change. Much of the right now sees the standard press as just the opposite, as a conduit and glorifier of protest and change and an irresponsible critic of officialdom.

One problem, of course, is that no standard image exists to crystallize when the word "press" is mentioned. Or for any other term describing journalism. When Spiro Agnew said "media monopoly" he plainly was thinking of the wicked *Washington Post* that owns one of two daily newspapers in Washington, one of ten television stations receivable in Washington and one of forty-four radio stations receivable in Washington. Apparently, Mr. Agnew, when he used such terms, was not thinking of the several hundred newspapers that endorsed him and Mr. Nixon and which control large chains, often owning the only newspaper and the only television station in their towns.

Furthermore, newspapers and broadcasting stations do differ one from the other. In some places they are the doctrinaire

[2] In *Caldwell v. U.S.* the Supreme Court held (June 1972) that a newsman does not have a First Amendment right to withhold information from a grand jury. Caldwell was a *New York Times* reporter who had succeeded in developing a number of contacts within the Black Panther Party. He was called to testify before a Federal grand jury about Panther affairs but refused to do so. He was cited for contempt and the case was prosecuted by the federal government. Other journalists have also been called to testify before grand juries recently.

enemy of change and in other places they are not. But since all institutions are under fire, it is inevitable that the whole class will feel this pressure.

The future of the press comes under question for yet another reason. The technology of communications is undergoing a change in our time that will have an impact comparable to the invention of movable type and of the telegraph. These developments will change society, the way people live, and inevitably they will change the nature of the handling of news. These changes involve the electronic reproduction of images and sounds, the computer, a national system of broadband cable connections to each home, and associated inventions.

Our news system as it exists today already is a formidable instrument for the distribution of daily social and political intelligence. Today it consists of 1,750 daily newspapers, 8,000 weeklies, 900 television stations and 7,200 radio stations. One way or another, these reach almost everyone. Newspapers probably reach 80 to 90 per cent of the population, television over 90 per cent and radio almost 100 per cent.

This is a communications network with power beyond anything experienced before in human history. With it, a total society can be mobilized, or at least its attention can be mobilized in seconds and minutes.

The most powerful leaders of the past—the Caesars, Genghis Khan, Alexander, Napoleon—could not reach their constituents except in weeks and months and then only through thousands of intermediaries.

Hitler taught us that radio can be used to obtain awesome masses of public attention. But it remained for television to make this vivid and overwhelming, a medium in which a leader can not only be heard, but can be seen and can reproduce reinforcing images to intensify his message and even to transmit emotions and messages that he dare not express in words.

At times of national emergencies the effectiveness of this system is remarkable. When John Kennedy was assassinated, 44 per cent of the American people knew it within fifteen minutes, 62 per cent knew it within thirty minutes, and 90 per cent within an hour. Half the people heard it through radio or television and they notified the other half by telephone or in person. Eighty-eight per cent of all households saw the 1968 Democratic convention, 95 per cent the Robert Kennedy funeral, 94 per cent the first moonwalk.

Think for a moment what this means. It isn't easy. Something profound has happened to the human race when 100 or 200 million human beings can all be made to think precisely the same thing at the same moment. What this means in potential mass action or political power is something we have only vaguely begun to consider.

We do know that it is an enormous commercial prize. The massed attention of the American audience is one of the most precious commodities in history. One minute of prime time television costs $65,000 but it buys access to 50 million brains. That's about one-eighth of a cent per brain—and looking at some of the commercials one sometimes feels that they may ultimately reduce the human brain to about that value.

So there is already a public communications system of unprecedented powers. Now there are about to be radical changes in the mechanics of the system that will change man and change his communications.

The crucial elements of this change are cable television and the computer. Cable, of course, is at present a substitute for television transmission through the air. Its original purpose was to serve rural areas too far from an existing transmitter or in mountainous places where television signals, which are relatively fragile, could not penetrate. Now it is extending into cities where big buildings make reception poor and where the inexpensive addition of extra channels provide more choices of programing than is available in the usual six through-the-air channels in the average big city.

Unfortunately, cable is still thought of by most people as merely an improvement in transmission of regular television, a better picture and maybe a slightly greater variety from distant cities. This is unfortunate because the real significance of cable lies elsewhere. It is an inexpensive way to bring a very large number of channels—forty or 100 or 200—into each home by wire. Over these capacious channels—each with more electronic capacity than 1,000 telephone lines—can be brought at very little cost messages from many places—library research, monitoring of public meetings, merchandising information, lectures from high schools and universities, personal presentations by local people and groups at almost no cost to themselves, and many other messages. Because it is a physical wire to each home, this means that the home can send a signal outward as well as receive one, and this gives the householder a choice over what he wants and when he wants it.

The computer is important to the system, not just because it is an enormously capacious calculator, but because it is also a master switching agent, memorizer, and can store words and images for rapid retrieval. It can understand the request of the citizen in his home, possibly transmitted from a home keyboard or maybe the pushbutton telephone dial, connect the home to the desired place, like a library, which will also be computerized, and direct images through its memory and switching to the particular home that called for them. It should not cost much if the right public policy on cable exists—maybe pennies per selection—and this would be computed as easily but less expensively than the telephone company now computes its billings.

Because this is based on wires to each home that can be combined by computers in an almost endless variety of interconnections, there can continue to be national and metropolitan networks, but there can also be networks which serve each small community and each neighborhood.

These and other developments will change how people deal with each other and with other societies. Communications satellites, hovering over a million square miles of earth, are infinitely cheaper than transoceanic and transcontinental cables. They receive signals sent upward to them and reflect them downward to the intended target area. Since it doesn't cost any more to reflect these signals across the continent than across the street, the cost of communications will begin to be unrelated to distance.

Home casettes, producing video programing analagous to

phonograph records, also seem likely, with all that means in educational, cultural and other pursuits.

Such changes have already started. Communications satellites have made live international video possible. Cable already is connected to four million homes and is expected to be connected to more than 90 per cent of all homes within eight years.

These will make a difference in the nature of journalism. Assume that the function of journalism is to provide the citizen with information he needs to understand and cope with his environment. This is a grandiose and in some ways pretentious definition of the journalist's function, because the whole human experience is directed at comprehending and dealing with this world. Certainly, journalism can't pretend that it is the only instrument for this. But it seems that this is the best guiding principle for the general goal of journalism. While it is obvious that many other human activities contribute to the individual's perceptions and grasp of his environment, journalism shares this function and should be complementary to the other methods.

Such a large goal for journalism is important for another reason. It helps explain why journalism in America is better today than it ever was but at the same time is still inadequate. This is so because the world has changed radically, and the impact of other kinds of communications has changed the perceptions of the human race. The individual today needs a different journalism than he did 100 years ago or even thirty years ago.

In a rural society when most people lived in small towns in a largely self-sufficient economy, what happened in distant places beyond their own first-hand knowledge was relatively unimportant. It is true that men declared war or levied taxes 1,000 miles away and these actions ultimately affected the villager. But the effect took a long time to reach him and in a non-participating, anti-democratic empire there wasn't much the citizen could do about it anyway.

The technological developments of the past changed journalism because it changed the way people saw their world. Movable type, the telegraph, the telephone, the steam train, the rotary press, the consumer economy—all these things changed the structure of society. They did not lessen the citizen's need for professional newsgathering but increased it, even though the citizen had new ways of getting information independent of the press. What happened, of course, was that society became organized in a highly interdependent way. Men no longer raised their own food and fabric. Their lives were immediately and profoundly affected by actions far away. They knew these actions were being taken and they were told they had a right to influence them.

Furthermore, the intensity of public action in the lives of individuals increased. The pieces of paper that the President signed not only declared war—at least in that dim, unremembered past when such archaic acts were performed—but they established rates of pay, the direction of highways, the nature of schooling. At the same time, the speed of communication accelerated social reaction time. Things happened faster and people couldn't wait to absorb the conventional wisdoms from their neighbors because what was happening was less and less conventional. They could not even depend on their parents because a lot of it was new to them, too. If a person were going to influence the policies that affected his or her life, that person had to know what was going on, what it meant and what actions could be taken before the policy was settled.

One of the reasons we live in a disturbed and dismaying time is that there exist ingenious ways of rapid communication from the great centers of institutions, including government and corporate life, outward to the population. But the means of explaining the significance and consequences of such policy decisions are inadequate and this is an inadequacy of journalism. And there are no counterpart methods to let the public react to policy constructively as rapidly as new policy is thrust upon them, which is an inadequacy of all political and social institutions.

The citizen of the future will have many new ways to obtain public information, some of this information now obtained through conventional journalism. The sense of interdependence of all peoples on the globe will grow, not necessarily with increased harmony. Fancy technology will make it increasingly clear that the average citizen needs to know more.

It may do something else. It may increase our already troubled lack of identity. We live in huge cities or in undifferentiated communities. We are a lonely crowd, moving into the cities like lemmings into the sea, because it is in the cities that we find institutions and social contact. But it is so overwhelming that we immediately have to find ways to screen most of it out. This paradox—the need to have human contact but finding ourselves overloaded with human contact beyond any reasonable level—has been worsened by the way the mass media are organized. A television station serves 10,000 square miles with the same program. It cannot possibly produce a sense of community and identity for the hundreds of communities within its single signal. Metropolitan newspapers cover similarly large areas and while it is easier for them to serve identifiable communities, they are still more homogenized than the units by which neighborhoods live.

This paradox has brought many reactions. There is a high level of neurosis and psychosis in cities. Some people react against it with communes, new communities, a rejection of megalopolis.

The media will have to deal with this paradox. It may be the reason why the largest single growth in printed media is the small weekly serving a small identifiable community. With cable, similar video networks that are of human, neighborhood dimensions will be possible.

Journalism also will have to change to meet the awareness that the citizen needs to know more. The citizen of the future will be even more educated and world-oriented than the one of today. He will learn directly of events through some of our media, such as television. And he will ask something else from other media, like print.

When sixty million people watch the presidential press conference at seven o'clock in the evening, they do not need the morning paper to inform them that the President had a press conference. What they need is to know what it meant and how it will affect their lives.

The ingenious communications of the future will not replace the journalist but it will demand a different kind of journalist, just as radio and television resulted in a journalist today who is unrecognizable from the average journalist of forty years ago. It used to be that the newspaperman who went to college was considered fatally flawed for the business, and he usually was. A serious interest in the subject matter of the news, with the possible exception of politics, was considered amateur. We forget that some of the heroes of the generation of journalists of the 1920's and 1930's were famous not because they were perceptive or accurate or knowledgeable but because they were able to write sensational stories based on questionable fragments of fact. William Randolph Hearst's major editor, Arthur Brisbane, once advised a promising reporter, "Never lose your superficiality," and that principle, in more pretentious terms, survives today on a distressing number of newspapers, though the number is decreasing.

Today's reporters are infinitely better prepared and more serious and better writers than any who came before them, and that includes young men and women on small as well as large papers. News people in broadcasting are better than ever, though their medium's constrictions drive them to frustration.

The journalist of the future will have to be more scholarly than he is today, he will have to know more, keep up with a wider range of literature, and have to write more clearly and profoundly. The audience will know more and more and demand all this accumulation of knowledge to be integrated.

But time is not compressible, at least so far. People will have no more time for news than they do today. Already the individual is inundated with more than he can possibly absorb. The quantity of scholarly and scientific knowledge is said to double every twelve years. Someone has to try to make sense of it for the average person or the non-professional who is interested. Someone has calculated that there are 1,800 advertising messages a day to which the average individual is exposed.

The new technology will help the future citizen select quickly what he wants from the growing ocean of information around

200

him. But he will need journalists of insight and intellectual discipline and clarity of writing to integrate it. The busy citizen will not tolerate muddy, poorly informed journalism when a turn of a dial or a moment at a keyboard will bring into his home a document or film clip of the most authoritative account in the world of whatever single subject he is interested in.

The future individual will not be concerned solely with the distant world any more than he is today. He will want to know what is happening in his school district and city hall. Locally as well as nationally, the journalist of the future will need more background and more discipline in discerning in local affairs what is important and what is not, and what its apparent significance is.

What has been described, of course, are the best journalists of today. These are men and women who work in a variety of styles and media, some subjective, some detached, some in multimedia, some in cold print, some Lester Markels and some Gay Taleses, some turning out cinema verite with hand-held cameras and some doing big institutional productions. Unless such variety continues, not only will life be very dull for both the journalist and the audience, but there will be no way to detect the inevitable arteriosclerosis that affects all established institutions. This is one impact of the lack of real competition in our media—some of our papers and broadcasting stations are dead but they don't know it yet and won't know it until some new medium arrives and signs the death certificate, even as television did for the old movie industry in the late 1940's.

Things could develop quite differently, of course. But one thing is certain—things will not remain the same and whatever the change, unless maximum freedom is maintained—freedom for the individual, freedom for ideas and new forms, freedom for the competition of ideas and institutions—the only environment in which a journalist can live and work, will be lost. And since change is inevitable, the reservoir of resources necessary to cope with change will also be lost because no one can safely predict which idea, no matter how strange it appears today, will not be urgently needed a generation from now.

201

All the fancy new techniques guarantee nothing but electronic virtuosity. Cables and printed circuits don't care who they work for or what message they carry. They can be used to increase diversity, individuality and harmony or they can be used to accelerate control, coercion and conformity. They are quite impartial.

So the future of journalism is not in the hands of the technologists and the social scientists and the city planners. It is in the hands of political leaders and the courts. And how the public, leaders, and courts emerge depends to a great degree on the determination of every journalist to remain free at any cost. This is crucial for journalists. But journalistic freedom is also a symbol and an instrument of general freedom without which the journalist has no future at all.

BEN BAGDIKIAN, the nation's foremost press critic, considers here the way journalism will travel in the near future. As he sees it, that way will be exceptionally difficult. There will be marvelous new machines, but journalists must learn to master them, lest the journalists be mastered. Even more difficult and dangerous are the increasing attempts of government to control journalism. The new information machines may well make this control even easier to attain. The chief protection or guard against this control will be the journalist who will fight to maintain his freedom, indeed to increase it, in the face of forces which would diminish it.

Bagdikian is presently the national correspondent for the Columbia Journalism Review. *He is a former assistant managing editor of the* Washington Post, *where he served as that paper's ombudsman. He is the winner of numerous awards and honors, including a George Foster Peabody award, Sidney Hillman Foundation award and a John Simon Guggenheim Foundation Fellowship. He is the author of several books, including* The Information Machines, The Shame of the Prisons *and* The Effete Conspiracy and Other Crimes By the Press.

A SELECTED
Bibliography

BOOKS

Agee, James and Walker Evans, *Let Us Now Praise Famous Men*, Houghton Mifflin, Boston, 1939.

Bagdikian, Ben H., *The Information Machines*, Harper and Row, New York, 1971.

Barron, Jerome, *Freedom of the Press for Whom?*, Indiana University Press, Bloomington, Indiana, 1973.

Barsam, Richard M., *Non-fiction Film: A Critical History*, E.P. Dutton, New York, 1973.

Breslin, Jimmy, *The World of Jimmy Breslin*, Viking Press, New York, 1967.

Capote, Truman, *In Cold Blood*, Random House, New York, 1965.

Carlson, Oliver, *The Man Who Made News: James Gordon Bennett*, Duell, Sloan, and Pearce, New York, 1942.

Charnley, Mitchell V., *Reporting*, Holt, Rinehart, Winston, New York, 1966.

Curtis, David, *Experimental Cinema*, Universe Books, New York, 1971.

Defoe, Daniel, *Journal of the Plague Year*, Oxford University Press, London, 1969.

Dennis, Everette, ed., *The Magic Writing Machine: Student Probes of the New Journalism*, University of Oregon School of Journalism, Eugene, Oregon, 1971.

Didion, Joan, *Slouching Toward Bethlehem*, Farrar, Straus and Giroux, New York, 1968.

Emery, Edwin H., *The Press and America*, Prentice-Hall, Englewood Cliffs, New Jersey, 1972.

Fang, I. E., *Television News*, Hastings House, New York, 1972.

Friendly, Fred W., *Due to Circumstances Beyond Our Control*, Random House, New York, 1967.

Glessing, Robert J., *The Underground Press in America*, Indiana University Press, Bloomington, Indiana, 1970.

Hazlitt, William, "The Fight," in *The Complete Works of William Hazlitt*, ed. P. P. Howe, J. M. Dent and Sons, London, 1933.

Hayes, Harold, *Smiling Through the Apocalypse: Esquire's History of the Sixties*, Dell, New York, 1971.

Hemingway, Ernest, *Green Hills of Africa*, Charles Scribner's Sons, New York, 1935.

Hersey, John, *The Algiers Motel Incident*, Alfred Knopf, New York, 1968.

Jacobs, Lewis, *The Documentary Tradition: From Nanook to Woodstock*, Hopkinson and Blake, New York, 1971.

Jacobs, Lewis, *The Emergence of Film Art*, Hopkinson and Blake, New York, 1969.

Johnson, Michael, *The New Journalism*, University of Kansas Press, Lawrence, Kansas, 1971.

Kael, Pauline, *Going Steady*, Little, Brown, Boston, 1970.

Korbluth, Jessie, ed., *Notes from the New Underground: An Anthology*, Viking Press, New York, 1968.

Liebling, A. J., *The Earl of Louisiana*, Simon and Schuster, New York, 1961.

Macdonald, Dwight, *Dwight Macdonald on Movies*, Prentice-Hall, Englewood Cliffs, New Jersey, 1969.

MacDougall, Curtis, *Interpretative Reporting*, Macmillan, New York, 1972.

McGinniss, Joe, *The Selling of the President 1968*, Trident Press, New York, 1969.

Mayer, Martin, *About Television*, Harper and Row, New York, 1972.

Mailer, Norman, *Advertisements for Myself*, New American Library, New York, 1960.

Mailer, Norman, *The Armies of the Night*, New American Library, New York, 1968.

Mailer, Norman, *Miami and the Siege of Chicago*, World Publishing Co., New York, 1968.

Mailer, Norman, *Of a Fire on the Moon*, Little, Brown, Boston, 1970.

Meyer, Philip, *Precision Journalism*, Indiana University Press, Bloomington, Indiana, 1973.

Mungo, Raymond, *Famous Long Ago: My Life and Hard Times with the Liberation News Service*, Beacon Press, Boston, 1970.

Orwell, George, *Down and Out in Paris and London*, V. Gollancz, London, 1933.

Orwell, George, *The Road to Wigan Pier*, V. Gollancz, London, 1937.

Renan, Sheldon, *An Introduction to the American Underground Film*, E. P. Dutton, New York, 1967.

Ross, Lillian, *Reporting*, Simon and Schuster, New York, 1964.

Royko, Mike, *Boss*, Dutton, New York, 1971.

Skornia, Harry J., *Television and the News*, Pacific Books, Palo Alto, California, 1968.

Stallman, R. W. and E. R. Hagemann, eds., *The War Dispatches of Stephen Crane*, New York University Press, New York, 1964.

Talese, Gay, *The Bridge*, Harper and Row, New York, 1964.

Talese, Gay, *Fame and Obscurity*, World Publishing Company, New York, 1970.

Talese, Gay, *Honor Thy Father*, World Publishing Company, New York, 1971.

Talese, Gay, *The Kingdom and the Power*, World Publishing Company, New York, 1969.

Twain, Mark, *The Innocents Abroad*, Macmillan, New York, 1929.

Thompson, Hunter, *Hell's Angels: A Strange and Terrible Saga*, Random House, New York, 1967.

Tyler, Parker, *Underground Film: A Critical History*, Grove Press, New York, 1969.

White, William, ed., *By-Line: Ernest Hemingway*, Charles Scribner's Sons, New York, 1967.

Wolfe, Tom, *The Electric Kool-Aid Acid Test*, Farrar, Straus and Giroux, New York, 1968.

Wolfe, Tom, *The Kandy-Kolored Tangerine-Flake Streamline Baby*, Farrar, Straus and Giroux, New York, 1965.

Wolfe, Tom, *The New Journalism*, with an anthology edited by Tom Wolfe and E. W. Johnson, Harper and Row, New York, 1973.

Wolfe, Tom, *The Pump House Gang*, Farrar, Straus and Giroux, New York, 1968.

Wolfe, Tom, *Radical Chic & Mau-Mauing the Flak Catchers*, Farrar, Straus, and Giroux, New York, 1970.

ARTICLES

Arlen, Michael J., "Notes on the New Journalism," *Atlantic*, May, 1972, pp. 43-47.

Balk, Alfred, James J. Kilpatrick, Nicholas Von Hoffman, Tom Wicker, Garry Wills, "Personal Involvement: A Newsman's Dilemma," *Quill*, June, 1972, pp. 24-32.

Balz, Daniel, "Want to see new journalism in newspapers? Well, don't hold your breath." *Quill*, September, 1972, pp. 18-21.

Boyer, Brian, "A Vision of the Kingdom and the Power to Come," *ASNE Bulletin*, January, 1972, pp. 13-17.

Brady, John, "Gay Talese: An Exclusive Interview," *Writer's Digest*, January, 1973, pp. 28-31.

Brown, Charles, "New Art Journalism Revisited," *Quill*, March, 1972, pp. 18-23.

Cahan, Erwin D., "Attica: A Question of Involvement," *ASNE Bulletin*, January, 1972, pp. 10-11.

Chase, Dennis, "From Lippmann to Irving to New Journalism," *Quill*, August, 1972, pp. 19-21.

Christianson, K. Scott, "The New Muckraking," *Quill*, July, 1972, pp. 10-15.

Deitch, David, "Change or Stagnation: The Case for Advocacy Journalism," *The Nation*, November 17, 1969, pp. 530-532.

Diamond, Edwin, " 'Reporter Power' Takes Root," *Columbia Journalism Review*, Summer, 1970, pp. 12-18.

Didion, Joan, "Alicia and the Underground Press," *Saturday Evening Post*, January 13, 1968, p. 14.

Gieber, Walter, "The Underground Press," *Grassroots Editor*, March-April, 1970, pp. 5-14.

Grant, Gerald "The 'new journalism' We Need," *Columbia Journalism Review*, Spring, 1970, pp. 12-16.

Hersey, John, "Hiroshima," *The New Yorker*, August 31, 1946, pp. 15-60.

Hodgson, Godfrey, "Radical Sex," *Washington Post*, July 1, 1973, pp. C1 and C5.

Hvistendahl, J. K., "The Reporter as Activist: A Fourth Revolution in Journalism," *Quill*, February, 1970, pp. 8-11.

Kirkpatrick, Clayton, "The New Propaganda," *ASNE Bulletin*, September, 1970, p. 28.

Lower, Elmer W., "Fairness and Balance in Television News Reporting," *Quill*, February, 1970, pp. 12-15.

Macdonald, Dwight, "Parajournalism, or Tom Wolfe and His Magic Writing Machine," *New York Review of Books*, August 26, 1965, pp. 3-5.

Macdonald, Dwight, "Parajournalism II: Wolfe and the *New Yorker*, *New York Review of Books*, February 3, 1966, pp. 18-24.

McGee, Frank, "TV Newsmen's Opinions on the Air?" *Senior Scholastic*, January 10, 1972, p. 19.

McHam, David, "The Authentic New Journalists," *Quill*, September, 1971, pp. 9-14.

McHam, David, ". . . Old Ain't Necessarily Good, Either!" *ASNE Bulletin*, January, 1972, pp. 3-6.

Markel, Lester, "Lester Markel: So What's New?" *ASNE Bulletin*, January, 1972, pp. 1; 7-9.

Masterson, Mark, "The New Journalism," *Quill*, February, 1971, pp. 15-17.

Montag, Tom, "Journalism," *Book Magazine*, May, 1973, pp. 23-31.

Newfield, Jack, "Is there a 'new journalism'?" *Columbia Journalism Review*, July- August, 1972, pp. 45-47.

Polner, Murray, "The Underground GI Press," *Columbia Journalism Review*, Fall, 1970, pp. 54-56.

Porter, William E., "Radicalism and the Young Journalist," *Saturday Review*, December 11, 1971, pp. 65-66.

Ridgeway, James, "The New Journalism," *American Libraries,* June, 1971, pp. 585-592.

Robinson, L. W., Harold Hayes, Gay Talese, and Tom Wolfe, "The New Journalism," *Writer's Digest,* January, 1970, pp. 32-35 and 19.

Self, Charles, "The New Journalism?" *Quill and Scroll,* December-January, 1973, pp. 10-11.

Tebble, John, "The Old New Journalism," *Saturday Review,* March 13, 1971, pp. 96-97.

"The Tribe is Restless," *Time,* July 18, 1969, p. 46.

Tomkins, Calvin, "Profiles: All Pockets Open," *The New Yorker,* January 6, 1973, pp. 31-49.

Von Hoffman, Nicholas, "The Four W's Approach—So Who Needs It," *ASNE Bulletin,* November, 1969, pp. 12-13.

Wakefield, Dan, "The Personal Voice and the Impersonal Eye," *Atlantic,* June, 1966, pp. 86-90.

Wolfe, Tom, "The Birth of the New Journalism; Eyewitness Report by Tom Wolfe," *New York,* February 14, 1972, pp. cover, 30-45.

Wolfe, Tom, "Lost in the Whichy Thicket," *New York,* April 18, 1965, pp. 16 ff.

Wolfe, Tom, "The New Journalism," *ASNE Bulletin,* September, 1970, pp. 1; 18-23.

Wolfe, Tom, "The New Journalism: A la Recherche des Whichy Thickets," *New York,* February 21, 1972, pp. 39-48.

Wolfe. Tom, "Tiny Mummies! The True Story of the Ruler of 43rd Street's Land of the Walking Dead," *New York,* April 11, 1965, pp. 7-9, 24-29.

Wolfe, Tom, "Why They Aren't Writing the Great American Novel Anymore," *Esquire,* December, 1972, pp. 152-159; 272-280.

Index

A. J. Liebling Counter-
Convention, 119
Accuracy, 44, 45, 84, 104, 145,
149, 150
Advertisements of Myself, 19
Advertising, 16, 102, 121, 122, 145,
175, 182, 183, 184, 185, 186, 195
Advocacy journalism, 10, 12, 13,
27, 59, 63, 65, 76, 81, 83, 86, 88,
89, 91, 92, 119, 140, 145
Agee, James, 60
Agnew, Spiro, 77, 120, 123, 179, 193
Alien and Sedition Acts, 192
Alsop, Joseph, 63
Alternative press, 94, 99, 104, 119
"Amateur" journalism, 24
American Report, 135
Anger, Kenneth, 164
Angle shooting, 142
Anthology Film Archives, 168
"Anticipation of the Night," 166
Areopagitica, 59
Arlen, Michael, 23
Armies of the Night, 20, 22, 23
Anderson, Jack, 61, 63
Anderson, Sherwood, 21
Arnett, Peter, 27
Associated Press, 23, 27, 59, 88,
147, 151
Association of Working Press, 118,
124
Atlantic, 23, 24
Avant-garde film, 162, 163

Bagdikian, Ben, 202
Bagehot, William, 24
Balanced journalism, 139, 154
Baldwin, James, 64
Baltimore (Evening) Sun, 141, 144
Barron, Arthur, 159
Barron, Jerome, 191
Beckett-Carpenter fight (G. B.
Shaw's coverage), 19
Berkeley Tribe (il.), 109
Between the Lines, 23
Bill of Rights, 173
Blacks and the media, 121, 156-157
Black Panthers, 96, 97, 99, 193
The Black Panther (il.), 98

Block structure (of writing), 21
Bonanno, Bill, 49, 50-58
Bonanno, Joseph, 47, 50-58
Bonanno (Profaci), Rosalie, 47,
50-58
Book, the, 42-49, book themes, 47
Boston, Ray, 24
Boswell, James, 80
Boyer, Brian, 104
Brakhage, Stan, 166, 168
Brennan, Justice, 189
Breslin, Jimmy, 22, 42, 61, 62
Bridge, The, 48
Brisbane, Arthur, 200
Broadcast media, 174, 175, 176, 177,
179, 181, 187, 188, 189, 200
Brown, Charles, 22
Brown, Robert, 47
Buckley, William F., 63
Buñuel, Luis, 164
*Business Executives' Move for
Vietnam Peace v. FCC*, 175
Byron, Lord, 22

"CBS Newshour," 152, 153
"CBS Reports," 152
CBS television, 95, 120, 145, 147, 148,
151, 152, 154, 155, 157, 158, 159,
176, 188
Cable television, 194, 195, 197, 199,
202
Caldwell v. U.S., 193
Canby, Vincent, 160
Cannon, Jimmy, 61, 62
Capote, Truman, 11, 19, 20, 22, 23,
61, 78
Catledge, Turner, 46
Censorship, 59, 172, 176, 179, 181,
184, 185, 192
Cezanne, 21
Chandler, Otis, 119
"Chelsea Girls, The," 168
Chicago (1968), 123, 124
Chicago American, 123, 124
Chicago Daily News, 121, 123, 126,
130, 131, 132, 133
Chicago Daily Planet, 100
Chicago Express, 132
Chicago Free Press, 104

Chicago Joint Board, Amalgamated Clothing Workers of America, AFL-CIO v. Chicago Tribune Company, 185
Chicago Journalism Review, 97, 104, 118, 123, 124, 127 (il.)
Chicago Seed, 99
Chicago Sun-Times, 97, 104, 120, 121, 122, 128, 131, 132, 134
Chicago Tribune, 97, 132, 134
"Chien Andalou, Un," 164
Cinema 16, 166
Cinema verite, 157, 201
Citizen response (via cable TV), 196, 198
Civil rights movement, 122
Clair, Rene, 164
Classified shopper, 100, 102
Cleaver, Eldridge, 59
Clutter murders, 19
Cocteau, Jean, 164, 166
Coles, Robert, 61
College press, 14, 100
Columbia Broadcasting System, Inc. v. Democratic National Committee, 190
Columbia Journalism Review, 202
Columns of opinion, 12, 16, columnists and commentators, 146
Communications satellites, 196, 197
Composite characterization (writing technique), 12, 26, 59, 80
Computers (and cable TV), 196
"Confession," 160
Conservatives (political right), 86, 193
Constitution, The (constitutional law), 173, 174, 177, 178, 181, 183, 184, 185, 187, 189
Contempt citations, 193
Conventional journalism, 86, 89, 91, 92, 94, 95, straight journalism, 140
Corruption of journalist, 20, 86
Cosmopolitan, 140
Costa-Gavras, 160
Counter press, 14
Cowan, Paul, 61
Crane, Stephen, 60
Creativity, 10
Cronkite, Walter, 149

Dali, Salvador, 164
Daniel, Clifton, 46, 47
Day, Benjamin, 26, 27
Defoe, Daniel, 11, 60
Degas, 21
Democracy in the newsroom, 11, 14, 15, 124, 144
Dennis, Everett, 11
Denver Post, 122
Deren, Maya, 164

Detroit Free Press, 104
Detroit Fifth Estate, 99
"Dairies, Notes and Sketches," 168
Didion, Joan, 62
Direct cinema, 157
Direct quotations, use of, 44, 45, 46, 47, 49
Documentary film, 15, 146, 152-159; news documentary, 155, 157; personal documentary, 156, 157, 158, 159
"Dog Star Man," 169 (il.), 170 (il.), 171
Dorfman, Ron, 124
Dos Passos, John, 21, 62
Drugs, 107, 113-117
Durst, Seymour, 67-75

"Eat," 167 (il.), 168
Editorial control, 141, 149
Ellsberg, Daniel, 180
Emerson, Thomas I., 177, 180, 182
Emery, Edwin, 22
"Empire," 168
"Entr'acte," 164
Esquire, 19, 23, 43, 47, 48, 49, 60
Establishment media, 94, 104, 171, 172, 201
Existentialism, 19, 20
Experimental cinema, 160, 164
Exploitational press, 100, 102

Fairness Doctrine, 16, 82, 174, 187
Family, 48
Fantasy, 48
Federal Communications Commission, 16, 146, 150, 158, 180
Federal Housing Administration, 95, 96
Felker, Clay, 60, 78, 80
Field V, Marshall, 120, 121, 185
"The Fight," 11, 18
Film, the, 14, 152, 153, 154, 160, 163, 171, 172; film equipment, 157, 164, 166
Film Culture, 166
Film-Makers Cooperative, 166
Film-Makers Cinematheque, 168
Film poetry, 162
"Fireworks," 164
First Amendment, 173, 174, 176, 177, 179, 180, 181, 182, 183, 184, 185, 186, 187, 191, 193
Flaherty, Robert, 156
Fourteenth Amendment, 173, 178
Fowler, Gene, 138
Fox, Thomas C., 135
Franklin, Benjamin, 27, 28
Freedom of the press, 173, 182, 185, 187, 188, 192, 193, 201, 202; of speech, 173, 178, 181, 183

209

Freeman, David, 80
Friendly, Fred, 152, 158, 179
Future trends (in journalism),
    192-202

Gatekeeper, 181
Gay liberation, 107-108
Goldstein, Al, 48
Graham, Katharine, 119, 180
"Great American Novel, The,"
    152, 159
Green Bay Press-Gazette, 184, 185
Green Hills of Africa, 11
Green, Larry, 130, 132, 133, 134
Gryphon Group, 166
"Guns of the Trees," 161 (il.)

Haight-Ashbury Free Press, 101 (il.)
Halberstam, David, 42, 61, 62
Hamill, Pete, 61, 62, 63
Hampton, Fred, 96, 97
Harper's, 20, 23
Harris, Richard, 87
Harry, 114 (il.)
"Harvest of Shame," 152
Hayes, Harold, 23, 47
Hazlitt, William, 11, 18, 19
Hearst, William Randolph, 27, 147,
    176, 200
Hecht, Ben, 103
Hefner, Hugh, 48
Hemingway, Ernest, 11
Hentoff, Nat, 87
Hersey, John, 60
Hersh, Seymour, 63, 89
Hitting and running (in news
    stories), 142
Honor America Day, 113-117
Honor Thy Father, 20, 45, 47, 48,
    49, 78

Identity crisis, 199
Ignoring the reader, 142-143
Imhoff, Ernest, 144
Impressionism, 21
In Cold Blood, 11, 19, 20, 78
Independent film, 162
Independent journalist, 93
Indochina Bulletin, 133
Institutional responsibility, 122
Internal monologue, 21, 44, 45
International News Service, 27
Interpretation (of News), 77, 78,
    83, 89
Inverted pyramid form (of news
    writing), 21, 79
Investigative reporting, 90, 91

Jaffe, Louis, 175, 176, 177, 179, 187
Jefferson, Thomas, 145
Jensen, Jay, 28

Jersey, Bill, 156
Johnson, Michael, 22
Johnson, Nicholas, 179
Journal of the Plague Year, A, 11
Journalism, function of, 197; need
    for, 198, 199, 200
Journalistic freedom, 10, 15, 16
Joyce, James, 171

Katz, Wilbur, 183
Kempton, Murray, 61
Keogh, Jim, 86, 87, 88
Kilpatrick, James Jackson, 86
Kingdom and The Power, The, 20,
    45, 46, 47, 48, 49, 78
Koop, Theodore, 151, 159

Lee, Phil, 138, 139
Let Us Now Praise Famous Men, 60
Letters to the Editor, 16, 182
Libel, 96, 182, 186, 188, 189
Liberals (political left), 86, 89, 193
Liberating influences, 10, 14, 15,
    160, 191
Liebling, A. J., 61
Life, 63
Lippmann, Walter, 155
Liston-Patterson fight (Mailer's
    coverage of), 19, 61
Literary journalism, 10, 11, 12, 23,
    27, 41, 119
Literary Times, 103, 104
Los Angeles Free Press, 99, 100
Los Angeles Times, 119, 134
"Louisiana Story," 156

Mafia, 43, 47, 49, 50-58, 78
Mailer, Norman, 11, 19, 20, 22, 23,
    60, 86
"Man of Aran," 156
Markel, Lester, 42, 44, 84, 201
Marx, Karl, 60
Mass Media, 85, 86, 91, 92, 105, 107,
    124, 146, 151, 153, 160, 174, 195
McCarthy, Joseph, 13, 64
McGinniss, Joe, 62
McLuhan, Marshall, 177
Media effects, 194
Media (journalism) reviews, 15,
    120, 123, 124
Media technology, 194, 200
Mekas, Jonas, 166, 168
Mencken, H. L., 61, 62
"Meshes of the Afternoon," 164
Miami and the Siege of Chicago,
    20, 23
Miller v. California, 171
Milton, John, 59
Minimizing detail (in news writing),
    143
Minow, Newton, 146

Mitchell, Joe, 61
Monet, 21
(more), 87, 120
Morgan, Tom, 60
Ms, 79
Muckraking, 61
Munsey, Frank, 83
Murrow, Edward R., 148, 152

Nader, Ralph, 90, 122
"Nanook of the North," 156
Nash, Jay Robert, 103, 104
Nation, 19, 86
National Inquirer, 100
National Observer, 100
National Organization of Women,
  178
National Review, 86
New American Cinema, 160, 162
New art of journalism, 22
New muckraking, 22, 90
New Journalism, 9, 10, 11, 12, 14, 15,
  16, 17, 19, 20, 21, 22, 23, 24, 25, 26,
  27, 28, 41, 42, 49, 59, 60, 61, 62,
  63, 64, 78, 79, 80, 81, 83, 84, 85,
  86, 87, 89, 90, 119, 138, 141, 144,
  145, 150, 151, 160, 163, 172, 191
New York, 26, 61, 63, 78
New York Herald Tribune, 22, 41,
  45, 59, 60
New York Post, 45, 120, 121, 122
New York Review of Books, 86, 104
New York Sun, 26, 27
New York Times, 20, 42, 43, 47, 48,
  49, 79, 84, 86, 87, 88, 89, 90, 91,
  92, 103, 119, 120, 126, 131, 134,
  135, 179, 193
New York Times v. Sullivan, 186, 187
New York Tribune, 60
New Yorker, 46, 61, 86
Newfield, Jack, 23, 43, 59, 65, 86, 88
News, 12, 27, 43, 76-77, 78, 88, 89,
  102, 104, 140, 147, 154, 157, 200
Newsweek, 86, 132, 133
Nixon, Richard, 64, 86, 87, 88, 89,
  90, 128, 129, 130, 134, 135, 136, 193
Non-fiction novel, 19, 78
Notes of a Native Son, 64

Objectivity, 13, 25, 28, 59, 63, 64,
  76, 77, 78, 82, 88, 145, 146, 150,
  151
  Objective journalism, 13, 17, 27,
    60, 63, 65, 83, 85, 89, 91, 92, 149,
    153, 159
Ortega y Gassett, 25
Orwell, George, 24, 60

Paine, Tom, 59

Paley, William, 149
Pegler, Westbrook, 61
Pentagon Papers, 63, 87, 90, 91, 96,
  103, 130, 134, 135, 179, 180, 192
Personal journalism, 59, 82, 145, 148,
  151; personalized journalism, 148
Personal vision for film, 163
Peterson, Sidney, 164
Phoenix (Boston), 100
Playboy, 60, 100, 140
Political purpose of film, 155
"Population Explosion, The," 152
Pound, Ezra, 21
Precision journalism, 11
Print media, 179, 182, 187, 189, 193,
  194, 199
Privacy, 186
Professionalism, 15, 88, 118, 119,
  124, 147, 149, 150, 151
Public access, 11, 14, 15, 16, 150,
  173-190, 191
Public Opinion, 174
Public rights, 16
Public television, 154
Pulitzer, Joseph, 22, 27, 146

Readers Digest, 63
Red Lion Broadcasting Co. v. FCC,
  174, 176, 188
Reed, Rex, 59, 61
"Reminiscences of a Journey to
  Lithuania," 165 (il.), 168
Renoir, 21
reporter, qualities of, 200, 201
Reston, James, 46, 88
Revolt of the Masses, 25
Ridgeway, James, 61
Right of reply, 182
Road to Wigan Pier, The, 25
Rock journalism, 22
Rolling Stone, 86, 100
Rosenau, Neal, 136-137
Rosenbloom v. Metromedia, 189
Rosenthal, A. M., 45
Ross, Lillian, 61
Ross, Thomas B., 128, 132
Royko, Mike, 61
Runyon, Damon, 138

Safer, Morley, 153
Salant, Richard, 148
San Francisco Chronicle, 122
Sandbagging, 141-142
Sandburg, Carl, 21
Schaap, Dick, 22, 42
Schiff, Dorothy, 120
Screw, 48, 100
Scripps, E. W., 27
Scripps-Howard, 176
"See It Now," 152

Seidenberg v. McSorley's Old Ale House, Inc., 178
"Selling of the Pentagon, The," 150
Semple Jr., Robert, 92
Sevareid, Eric, 146
Sex in America (Talese), 48
Sexploitation films, 108-113
Shaw, George Bernard, 11, 19
Shawn, William, 60
Sheehan, Neil, 90
Sheehy, Gail, 26
Shelley, Percy B., 22
Sinatra, Frank, 46, 60
"Sixteen in Webster Groves," 154, 159
"60 Minutes," 159
Small, William, 145, 146
Smith, Jack, 160
Sol, El, 25
"Songs," 171
State Action problem, 173, 174, 176, 177, 178, 183, 184, 185, 189
"State of Siege," 160
Stanton, Frank, 149
Steffens, Lincoln, 61, 62
Steinbeck, John, 62
Steinem, Gloria, 79
Stone, I. F., 61, 119
Sulzberger, Arthur, Ochs, 46, 119, 180
Supreme Court, 173, 174, 180, 186, 187, 188, 189, 192, 193

Talese, Gay, 17, 20, 21, 22, 49, 60, 61, 78, 79, 80, 84, 120, 160, 201
Tarbell, Ida, 61
Television, 89, 90, 145-151, 175, 181, 187, 193, 194, 195, 199
Terkel, Studs, 61
Theophrastus, 26
Time, 86, 140
"Time for Burning, A," 156
Tisch, Robert, 67-75
To Kill A Messenger, 145, 146

Tornillo v. Miami Herald, 190
Traditional journalism, 13, 17
Twain, Mark, 11, 42, 60, 84

Underground film, 158, 160, 162-172; criticism of, 166, 168; distribution of, 166, 168, 172; forms, 162, 163; future of, 171, 172
Underground journalism, 11, 14, 15, 22, 62, 93, 97, 100, 104
Underground press, 93, 94, 100, 103, 105, 171; page design, 105; subject matter, 107; writing, 107
Underground radio, 22
United Press, 27, 88, 147
Unsafe At Any Speed, 90

Vidal, Gore, 22
Video casettes (home), 196
Vietnam, 94, 97, 99, 125-136, 153, 158, 192
Village Voice, 60, 63, 65, 66 (il.), 87
Voltaire, 59

Wakefield, Dan, 23, 26
Warhol, Andy, 160, 168
Washington Post, 9, 10, 41, 119, 120, 131, 134, 179, 193, 202
"Webster Groves Revisited," 154, 159
White, Justice, 188
White, William Allen, 83
Wicker, Tom, 61, 87, 119, 124
Wolf, Dan, 60
Wolfe, Tom, 12, 17, 18, 19, 21, 22, 23, 26, 41, 42, 49, 60, 61, 62, 78, 79, 80, 88, 160
Woodward III, William, 120
Wulf, Melvin, 187

Yellow journalism, 27, 145

"Z," 160